To The Instructor

■

Who Are We? presents brief readings on two related pairs of themes—identity and community, and work and career—that appear as possible topic choices in all of the assignment chapters in the *St. Martin's Guide to Writing*, fifth edition. We hope that these themes will resonate for your students, as they have for our own students and for the students of instructors who advised us on this project. Students will find these themes not only relevant to their personal concerns and aspirations, but also socially and culturally significant. The voices in these readings echo many of the voices in America today. They rejoice in the promise that is America, while recognizing that for many the American dream—as Langston Hughes, with whom this anthology begins and ends, so eloquently writes—is still a "dream deferred."

We designed *Who Are We?* with minimal apparatus so that it could be used with any rhetoric or handbook to help students learn to think critically while learning new composing and discursive practices. It contains two parts, "Identity and Community" and "Work and Career." Each part begins with a brief introduction suggesting some of the ways the readings develop the theme, and each reading is preceded by a headnote inviting students to join in the conversation.

The idea for a compact thematic reader arose as we introduced thematic topics into the *St. Martin's Guide to Writing*. (In each assignment chapter's "Guide to Writing," these special topics may be found early in the "Invention" or "Invention and Research" section, where they appear under separate headings as alternatives to more general topics.) We wanted to offer instructors a collection of readings on the two themes that would complement students' work on the assignments in the *Guide*. Here we offer a few practical suggestions for integrating the readings in *Who Are We?* into a course in which instructors are using the *St. Martin's Guide*.

- To interest students in choosing essay topics from either theme, begin your course by discussing one or two readings about each theme.
- To prepare students to follow a theme throughout the course, begin by discussing several readings about that theme.
- To enrich written responses to or discussion of a "Connecting to Culture and Experience" activity following a *Guide* reading, assign a thematically relevant reading.
- To broaden students' topic choices for either theme, mine the readings for topic possibilities.
- To deepen written responses to and discussion of a "Considering the Social Dimensions" activity at the very end of each chapter in Part 1 of the *Guide*, assign a relevant reading.
- To broaden students' experience with a genre in the *Guide*, assign a reading in the same genre — for example, a profile when students are analyzing writing strategies for profiles (Chapter 4 in the *Guide*).
- If you assign Chapter 5, Explaining a Concept, ask students to write about one of the thematic concepts, such as "identity," using relevant readings as source materials.
- If you assign Chapter 6, Arguing a Position, encourage students to take positions on issues raised by the readings.
- If you assign Chapter 8, Justifying an Evaluation, ask students to evaluate the logic, emotional manipulation, or credibility of an argument reading. (Chapter 12 offers guidelines for such an evaluation.)
- If you assign Chapter 10, Interpreting Stories, encourage students to interpret one of the short stories in *Who Are We?* or to adopt an idea about identity, community, work, or career in the readings as a basis for interpreting a story.
- If your students prepare a portfolio at the end of a course in which they have followed one of the thematic strands, invite them to make use of ideas in the readings to deepen their insights about what they have learned during the course.

You and your colleagues will undoubtedly discover further strategies for bringing these two valuable, complementary texts together. For example, using these suggestions — and others — instructors could conceivably create in their classrooms complete reading and writing workshops, in which students could analyze, synthesize, and evaluate ideas on common topics for real rhetorical situations and purposes. Using the readings, students might examine a particular problem in their community through a series of autobiographical, explanatory, and argumentative essays, or they might combine themes, for instance, exploring how their own and others' sense of identity and self-worth is affected by the kinds of work they do now or hope to do in the future. For more suggestions on ways to use *Who Are We?* visit our Web site at <http://www.smpcollege.com/theGuide/instructor.html>.

We want to thank the instructors and students who have used our books and taught us so much in the process. In particular, we are grateful to the following instructors and their students for helping us formulate these themes: Saralinda Blanning, Wright State University; Richard Boyd, University of California at Riverside; James Brown, Kansas City Kansas Community College; Richard Bullock, Wright State University; Joan Kuzma Costello, Inver Hills Community College; Judith M. Davis, The Catholic University of America; Tamara Dozier, Wright State University; Nancy Etheridge, Boise State University; Judith Gardner, University of Texas at San Antonio; Tammy Metcalf, Wright State University; Michael Miller, Longview Community College; Victoria Sarkisian, Marist College; Lee Smith, University of Houston; James H. Wilson, Santa Fe Community College; Rosemary Winslow, Catholic University of America; and Stacy Wolkwitz, Wright State University. We want especially to thank four people who made a special contribution to the development of this book: Kathryn O'Rourke, California State University at San Bernardino; Stephanie Kay, University of California at Riverside; Steven Gould Axelrod, University of California at Riverside; and Jeremiah B. Axelrod, University of California at Irvine. As always, we are enormously indebted to the caring and professional people at St. Martin's Press, especially Carla Samodulski, Meg Spilleth, Jessica Zorn, Donna Erickson, and Steve Debow.

Charles dedicates the "work and career" readings to his students who must work in order to go to college. These students' stories always remind him of the varied part-time jobs he held as a college student in the 1950s: washing pots and pans in the college cafeteria, collecting trash in the dormitories, taking phone calls at the dormitory's reception desk, operating a copy machine in the library, driving an early-morning bakery delivery truck, and weighing full and then empty trailers at a cotton gin on the night shift. A welcome contrast to solitary study, these short-term jobs were purposeful social events that required close coordination with fellow workers and others.

Rise would like to dedicate this book to the memory of her father, Alexander Borenstein, who taught her that you know yourself both by the work you do and the sense of solidarity you share with others.

Rise B. Axelrod

Charles R. Cooper

Who Are We?

Readings on Identity,
Community,
Work, and Career

RISE B. AXELROD
University of California, Riverside

CHARLES R. COOPER
University of California, San Diego

Bedford/St. Martin's
Boston ♦ New York

Sponsoring editor: Donna Erickson
Director of development, English: Carla Samodulski
Development editor: Meg Spilleth
Managing editor: Patricia Mansfield Phelan
Editorial assistant: Jessica Zorn
Production supervisor: Joe Ford
Art director/Cover design: Lucy Krikorian

Library of Congress Catalog Card Number: 97-65638

Manufactured in the United States of America.

6   5   4   3
f

For information, write:
Bedford/St. Martin's
75 Arlington Street
Boston, MA 02116
(617-399-4000)

ISBN: 0-312-15717-7

Acknowledgments

CONTENTS

.

vii

Contents

Contents

A journalist profiles teenagers who believe that identity is a cultural choice we can make for ourselves.

> For April and her friends, identity is not a matter of where you come from, what you were born into, what color your skin is. It's what you wear, the music you listen to, the words you use—everything to which you pledge allegiance, no matter how fleetingly.

A professor studying social psychology and technology profiles Multi-User Dungeons, or MUDs, sites on the Internet at which people assume different identities and form virtual communities.

> A MUD can become a context for discovering who one is and wishes to be. In this way, the games are laboratories for the construction of identity. . . . The culture of simulation may help us achieve a vision of a multiple but integrated identity whose flexibility, resilience, and capacity for joy comes from having access to our many selves.

A psychotherapist argues that instead of creating a color-blind global village, the Internet may have the effect of increasing rather than diminishing fear and racism.

> While racist assumptions arguably are deep and institutionalized, there also may be simpler culprits: limited experience with people outside of one's own ethnic group and false reasoning. . . . The technology only reinforces the barriers in my life that prevent me from meeting and interacting with people.

A sociologist explains the concept of community as it has traditionally been understood and as it is currently being revised for the multicultural and technological America of the twenty-first century.

> America does not need a simple return to gemeinschaft, to the traditional community. . . . In short, we need new communities in which people have choices and readily accommodate divergent *sub*communities but still maintain common bonds.

This classic story shows what evil can be done for the common good.

> Mr. Graves opened the slip of paper and there was a general sigh through the crowd as he held it up and everyone could see that it was blank. Nancy

and Bill, Jr., opened theirs at the same time, and both beamed and laughed, turning around to the crowd and holding their slips of paper above their heads.

A communications professor analyzes four elements of gay community building: the establishment of neighborhoods or common turf, social groups, symbols, and meeting behavior.

> Lesbians and gay men . . . are creating a new community in the midst of the American melting pot. They are building social organizations, exercising political power, and solidifying a unique sense of identity—often under repressive and sometimes dangerous conditions.

Education professors George D. Kuh and Ernest T. Pascarella, along with Henry Wechsler, the director of Harvard's College Alcohol Studies Program, propose reforms to encourage diversity in fraternities.

> In terms of race, ethnicity, and sexual orientation, fraternities tend to be more homogeneous than the student body in general. This is borne out by other data from the National Study of Student Learning. They show that, during the first year of college, fraternity and sorority members make significantly smaller gains than non-members do on measures of openness to diversity, which include valuing contact with people from different backgrounds and learning about people from different cultures.

PART II. WORK AND CAREER 93

A poet celebrates the joy of doing work that is "real."

> The work of the world is common as mud.
> Botched, it smears the hands, crumbles the dust.
> But the thing worth doing well done
> has a shape that satisfies, clean and evident. . . .
> The pitcher cries for water to carry
> and a person for work that is real.

Contents

The labor market is sending a clear signal. While the American way of moving youngsters from high school to the labor market may be imperfect, the chief problem is that, for many, even getting a job no longer guarantees a decent standard of living. More than ever, getting ahead, or even keeping up, means staying in school longer.

"They called us the Green Machine," says Jason Pratt, recently retired McDonald's griddleman, " 'cause the crew had green uniforms then. And that's what it is, a machine. You don't have to know how to cook, you don't have to know how to think. There's a procedure for everything and you just follow the procedures."

What the survey does not show is the suppressed rage of workers who tolerate abuses and absurdities in a marketplace leaned-and-meaned to Wall Street specifications. Reading "Dilbert" allows them, in some small way, to strike back, or at least to experience a pleasant catharsis by identifying the nature of the beast: a general yet pervasive sense of idiocy in corporate America that is seldom dealt with by the captains of industry who have great hair and offices with doors.

Americans take individualism seriously. They are personally responsible for their own failures. They have no right to expect help from others. Anything given by others is an act of charity, not required, and ultimately demeaning to those who get it.

Technically, of course, all workers in the United States . . . have the right to organize and bargain collectively with their employers, but, as a waitress in Las Vegas points out, "you say the word *union* in a non-union place and you get fired. If you want to organize, you're really putting your neck on the line."

Contents

A poet expresses disappointment and frustration that the American dream has not yet been realized for many Americans, but he continues to look with hope toward the future.

O, let America be America again—
The land that never has been yet—
And yet must be—the land where *every* man is free.
The land that's mine—the poor man's, Indian's, Negro's, ME—
Who made America,
Whose sweat and blood, whose faith and pain,
Whose hand at the foundry, whose plow in the rain,
Must bring back our mighty dream again.

IDENTITY AND COMMUNITY

Who Are We? *This is the question many of us are asking. We want to know who we are as individuals and as a community. The readings in Part I challenge and encourage us to think deeply about this question.*

The first group of readings looks critically at race as a defining factor in identity. Beginning with "Theme for English B" by Langston Hughes, race is seen as a mark of difference that sets people apart while also making them a part of a community with a shared history and culture. John S. Pitt complains in "Don't Call Me Red" about stereotyping, the practice of assuming that superficial qualities such as hair or skin color reveal a person's true nature. "Growing Up Asian in America" tells how stereotyping impelled Kesaya E. Noda to forge her own sense of identity by rediscovering her racial and cultural roots.

Next, we read about how our sense of who we are is affected by gender roles and expectations. Psychologist Ellyn Kaschak explains in "The Prism of Self-Image" that children's sense of gender identity and self-worth develops from the way they see themselves reflected in the eyes of others. Kaschak's theory is illustrated in Marge Piercy's poem "Barbie Doll" and H. G. Bissinger's profile "Dreaming of Heroes." Piercy suggests what can happen to women who measure themselves against society's ideal of feminine beauty. Bissinger shows how a boy's desire to live up to the heroic expectations of his dead father can be truly inspiring. In contrast, Jenny Lyn Bader says in "Larger Than Life" that young people have lowered their expectations and no longer believe in heroes.

The next two selections, "Goin' Gangsta, Choosin' Cholita: Claiming Identity" by Nell Bernstein and "Who Am We?" by Sherry Turkle, invite us to look at identity from a different, postmodern perspective. The postmodern view contrasts with the more traditional ways of thinking about identity that we have seen in the preceding readings. Traditionally, identity is regarded as a matter of nature or nurture—or some combination of the two. We can see the nature theory

"It's a baby. Federal regulations prohibit our
mentioning its race, age, or gender."

Drawing by P. Steiner; ©1996 The New Yorker Magazine, Inc.

*motivating Noda's search for identity in her racial heritage. Kaschak's essay, on
the other hand, is based on the idea that nurture is the determining factor. She
argues that what we think it means to be a particular gender is not innate but
learned—engendered or socially constructed, as she puts it. The postmodern view
of identity regards categories such as race and gender as flexible, rather than fixed,
more a matter of choice than of either nature or nurture. Bernstein, for example,
shows a group of teenagers who believe they can adopt a different racial identity
simply by changing their clothes and way of speaking. Similarly, Turkle shows
how in cyberspace, where people can assume many different identities, gender is
simply another role to perform.*

*These different ways of thinking about identity lead us in the pieces that
follow to consider who we are not only as individuals but also as a community. For
Turkle, the new freedom and flexibility of cyberspace promises a greater sense of
community as people are freed from their narrow identities and better able to
empathize with others who have different experiences and points of view. Dorothy*

Chin, on the other hand, argues in "The Internet Encourages Isolation" that the computer age may actually have the opposite effect as we spend more and more time by ourselves and less time face-to-face with other people.

The next two readings by Amitai Etzioni and Shirley Jackson take up the debate about what the community of the future should look like. In "The New Community," Etzioni proposes that we build a new American community by encouraging the development of many subcommunities that allow people to express their unique identities yet share common bonds and goals. Jackson's classic story "The Lottery" suggests that communities in which everyone knows each other may be just as pernicious as cities in which people don't know their neighbors.

Our discussion concludes with case studies of two subcommunities. The first, "America's Emerging Gay Culture" by Randall E. Majors, analyzes the patterns of communication that help to build and consolidate the gay community within the context of a primarily heterosexual society. The second, "The Questionable Value of Fraternities" by George Kuh, Ernest Pascarella, and Henry Wechsler, sees a problem in the homogeneity of fraternities and sororities on college campuses for society at large as well as for the individual members. The writers argue that while members may benefit from the support and sense of belonging they gain from the clubs, they also lose out on an important opportunity to get to know a greater diversity of people.

THEME FOR ENGLISH B

Langston Hughes

■

A PROLIFIC WRITER, LANGSTON HUGHES may be best known for his influential role in the Harlem Renaissance, the great intellectual and artistic flowering of African American culture in the 1920s. In "Theme for English B," which was originally published in 1959, Hughes tells the familiar story of a student trying to write something that reveals his "true" or authentic self. College instructors have been making this kind of assignment ever since Socrates urged his own students in the fifth century B.C. to "know thyself." But as Hughes's speaker observes, "It's not easy to know what is true" about yourself.

Part of the difficulty comes from the way we define ourselves. For the speaker in the poem, race is a defining category. Not only does it identify who he is, but it also marks the difference between himself and his "white" instructor.

Hughes also reflects on race in his autobiography The Big Sea *(1940). In it, he explains that although as Americans we tend to emphasize our racial differences, the category of race is not "pure" as it is in Africa: "In the United States, the word 'Negro' is used to mean anyone who has any Negro blood at all in his veins." Hughes describes himself as quintessentially American, tracing his ancestry to African slaves as well as to Native American Indians (Cherokee) and Scottish, Jewish, English, and French immigrants.*

Words like hybrid, mestizo, *and* multicultural *are used by some people to describe the complexities of racial identity. Whatever word you choose, telling the truth about who you are requires you to critically examine categories such as race, gender, class, religion, and sexual orientation. As you read "Theme for English B," think about how these categories are being used and what they*

4

*imply about how we define ourselves as individuals and relate to one another
as members of a community.*

The instructor said,

> *Go home and write*
> *a page tonight.*
> *And let that page come out of you —*
> *Then, it will be true.*   5

I wonder if it's that simple?
I am twenty-two, colored, born in Winston-Salem.
I went to school there, then Durham, then here
to this college on the hill above Harlem.
I am the only colored student in my class.   10
The steps from the hill lead down into Harlem,
through a park, then I cross St. Nicholas,
Eighth Avenue, Seventh, and I come to the Y,
the Harlem Branch Y, where I take the elevator
up to my room, sit down, and write this page: 15

It's not easy to know what is true for you or me
at twenty-two, my age. But I guess I'm what
I feel and see and hear, Harlem, I hear you:
hear you, hear me — we two — you, me, talk on this page.
(I hear New York, too.) Me — who?   20

Well, I like to eat, sleep, drink, and be in love.
I like to work, read, learn, and understand life.
I like a pipe for a Christmas present,
or records — Bessie, bop, or Bach.
I guess being colored doesn't make me *not* like   25
the same things other folks like who are other races.
So will my page be colored that I write?
Being me, it will not be white.
But it will be
a part of you, instructor.   30
You are white —
yet a part of me, as I am a part of you.
That's American.

Sometimes perhaps you don't want to be a part of me.
Nor do I often want to be a part of you.   35
But we are, that's true!
As I learn from you,
I guess you learn from me —
although you're older — and white —
and somewhat more free.   40

This is my page for English B.

DON'T CALL ME RED

John S. Pitt

■

WHILE LANGSTON HUGHES DEFINES HIMSELF by the color of his skin, corporate-training specialist John S. Pitt writes about being stereotyped by others because of the color of his hair. To some readers, Pitt's complaint may seem trivial. However, the editors of Newsweek, *who originally published his essay in their "My Turn" column (October 1996), agree with Pitt's assertion that "millions of people" are frustrated by our society's tendency to place a "greater emphasis on appearance than on accomplishment."*

Before reading Pitt's essay, you might pause to think about stereotyping. Pitt mentions a few common stereotypes—fat people are jolly, white men can't jump—and one that affects him most personally—all redheads are clowns. Think of stereotypes you believe, and consider why you believe them. Rather than speculating on the cultural or psychological causes of stereotyping, Pitt explains its effect on him. Why do you suppose stereotyping can affect one's sense of identity? What does it matter what others think?

Assuming that many readers will be unaware of the kind of stereotyping he has experienced, Pitt cites examples to make readers see how pervasive stereotyping of redheads as "cute and funny" is in contemporary culture. As you read "Don't Call Me Red," note how many of his examples you recognize. It has been suggested that Pitt is not really serious but is parodying people who complain about being stereotyped. What in the essay might contribute to this impression?

Ohhhh, a redhead," my mother sighed with delight the moment I was born. Sometime later she determined that I was also a blue-   1

7

eyed, male child. My hair color has been my predominant physical feature ever since. I've had red hair for 34 years now, yet many people I know still can't get used to it. They continually remind me of its peculiarity. What's more, they fully expect my behavior to be as quirky as my pate.

I'm not alone. I've found that many people react to redheads the same way. They assume we are all clowns. And who can blame them? Every redhead they have ever seen on TV or in the movies has been a comedian. Famous redheads don't fall in love or save the day. They just waddle around in baggy pants and shove handfuls of chocolates into their mouths. As a result, real-life redheads of every demeanor and personality must strive to forge identities apart from Bozo and Lucy. Aren't all redheads funny like Red Skelton . . . crazy like Carol Burnett . . . or outrageous like Charo? Obviously not, but it's amazing how quickly a child called carrot-top learns to act silly.

I bristled every time someone called me Rusty or Red or Ronald McDonald, but I played the part well. I clowned for my elementary-school peers, then cursed my hair color at home. My parents told me I was lucky to have red hair. They said it was special. I didn't see anything lucky or special about it. I hated it. The only thing that infuriated me more than the taunting I received was the pandering. Elderly relatives and passersby patted the top of my amber head and called me cute. They said I looked just like little Jody on TV's "Family Affair," then they would chuckle to themselves. I didn't want to be cute and funny like Jody. I wanted to be dashing and rugged like Johnny Quest.

My hair color continued to be a defining factor in my life as I grew from the cheerful Jody stage into the awkward Danny Partridge stage. "Hey, Red, where'd ya get that hair?" I was asked 10,000 times. "I'm Kris Kringle's secret love child," came my obnoxious teen reply. It was exactly the kind of response people wanted from me. They didn't interpret it as biting or resentful. It was cute and funny.

I couldn't make myself be taken seriously. My sophomore oration on apartheid in South Africa was deemed to be "commendable" and "well researched," but my humorous reading of "Yertle the Turtle" earned the highest marks. I tried out for the menacing part of Dracula in the school play (granted, I didn't have the jet-black widow's peak, but my skin was sufficiently pale). Instead, I was cast as the funny lab assistant who runs from bats and screams a lot.

Like some suicidally self-conscious demon, I swore that the Curse of the Cute and Funny Redhead would end with me. I vowed that I would never marry a redhead. I knew that a redheaded couple was bound to have redheaded children and that was a fate I naturally wouldn't wish on anyone, especially my own kids.

Through the Happy Days of high school, I stubbornly dated only blond and brunette girls, hoping that they would see me as more than Ralph Malph or Richie Cunningham. Their autographs in my senior yearbook confirmed that they did not; "Dear John, you are so cute and funny . . . have a nice life."

I maintained my self-imposed ban on redheaded relationships until I was 25. Then, to nobody's surprise but my own, I fell head over heels in love with a beautiful redhead. Happily, she fell for me in spite of her own vow to avoid Rusty relationships. As a redheaded girl named Wendy, she'd also had her fill of being compared to hamburger-chain icons. We have been married for nine years now and are the parents of three children. "Oh, a redhead," we sighed in delighted unison the moment each was born.

Now my wife and I must convince our children that red hair is lucky and special. Our goal is to help them take pride in themselves and find their own identities, separate from Krusty the Clown or Dennis Rodman on a red day. This is no easy task.

A family of five brunettes can enter a busy restaurant or walk down a crowded grocery aisle without generating a hint of interest, but put a family of redheads on the scene and it is as though the Ringling brothers . . . and Barnum . . . and Bailey are on parade. People stop, stare and even point.

"Well, I wonder where they got all that red hair?" we are asked whenever anybody makes the alarming discovery that the three redheaded children in the shopping cart belong to the two redheaded adults standing nearby. "We have no idea . . . we found them under a giant cabbage near Chernobyl" is the answer we'd like to give. Instead we just smile and say, "They're all ours, thank you." "Wow, I bet there's never a dull moment around your house," comes their presumptive reply.

As proud parents we are frustrated that people focus more attention on our children's hair color than on who they are and what they do. It is the same frustration held by millions of people in a society that places greater emphasis on appearance than on accomplishment.

"Oh, yes, he's the bald guy who . . ." or "You know, that short woman who . . ." are examples of all too common introductory phrases that fill our vernacular and open the door to stereotypes of all sorts. The truth is that not all obese people are jolly and not all redheads are clowns in baggy pants—and some white men can jump.

My children are still young. They have yet to encounter all the preconceptions that come with having red hair, but they soon will. They will also develop the sense of humor it takes to roll with the jokes, the remarks and the comparisons to silly characters. I just hope that their humor evolves as a natural and pleasant extension of who they are, and not as a forced response to society's need for another clown.

GROWING UP ASIAN IN AMERICA

Kesaya E. Noda

■

LIKE LANGSTON HUGHES AND JOHN S. PITT, Kesaya E. Noda writes about stereotyping and the search for identity. "Growing Up Asian in America," which first appeared in Making Waves: An Anthology of Writings by and about Asian American Women *(1989), tells Noda's moving personal story. She explains that as a Japanese American child growing up in New Hampshire she felt doubly alienated—from her neighbors whose stereotypes made her feel "unalterably alien" and from her racial heritage that seemed to force itself upon her and "paste itself right to [her] face."*

As a student of religion with degrees from Harvard Divinity School and Harvard University, Noda recognizes that she needed to look inward to find herself. But she also had to look beyond herself to rediscover her roots "in community . . . culture and history." Noda's quest takes her to Japan where she claims her racial inheritance by learning the language, culture, and religion. Then it takes her to California where she learns firsthand what life was like for Japanese American immigrants like her grandparents. (She doesn't mention it, but Noda's research led her to write a history of her grandparents' farming community, The Yamato Colony, *published in 1981.) Finally, Noda's quest takes her home to her mother where she discovers part of being herself is being her mother's daughter, a Japanese American woman.*

As you read Noda's essay, think about the historical influences and cultural traditions that contribute to your sense of who you are. What elements combine to form your identity?

S ometimes when I was growing up, my identity seemed to hur- 1
tle toward me and paste itself right to my face. I felt that way, encoun-

tering the stereotypes of my race perpetuated by non-Japanese people (primarily white) who may or may not have had contact with other Japanese in America. "You don't like cheese, do you?" someone would ask. "I know your people don't like cheese." Sometimes questions came making allusions to history. That was another aspect of the identity. Events that had happened quite apart from the me who stood silent in that moment connected my face with an incomprehensible past. "Your parents were in California? Were they in those camps during the war?" And sometimes there were phrases or nicknames: "Lotus Blossom." I was sometimes addressed or referred to as racially Japanese, sometimes as Japanese-American, and sometimes as an Asian woman. Confusions and distortions abounded.

How is one to know and define oneself? From the inside — within a context that is self-defined, from a grounding in community and a connection with culture and history that are comfortably accepted? Or from the outside — in terms of messages received from the media and people who are often ignorant? Even as an adult I can still see two sides of my face and past. I can see from the inside out, in freedom. And I can see from the outside in, driven by the old voices of childhood and lost in anger and fear. 2

I Am Racially Japanese

A voice from my childhood says: "You are other. You are less than. You are unalterably alien." This voice has its own history. We have indeed been seen as other and alien since the early years of our arrival in the United States. The very first immigrants were welcomed and sought as laborers to replace the dwindling numbers of Chinese, whose influx had been cut off by the Chinese Exclusion Act of 1882. The Japanese fell natural heir to the same anti-Asian prejudice that had arisen against the Chinese. As soon as they began striking for better wages, they were no longer welcomed. 3

I can see myself today as a person historically defined by law and custom as being forever alien. Being neither "free white," nor "African," our people in California were deemed "aliens, ineligible for citizenship," no matter how long they intended to stay here. Aliens ineligible for citizenship were prohibited from owning, buying, or leasing land. They did not and could not belong here. The voice in me remembers that I am always a *Japanese*-American in the eyes of many. A third-generation German-American is an American. A third-generation Japanese-American is a Japanese-American. Being Japanese means being a dan- 4 ger to the country during the war and knowing how to use chopsticks. I wear this history on my face.

I move to the other side. I see a different light and claim a different context. My race is a line that stretches across ocean and time to link me to the shrine where my grandmother was raised. Two high, white banners lift in the wind at the top of the stone steps leading to the shrine. It is time for the summer festival. Black characters are written against the sky as boldly as the clouds, as lightly as kites, as sharply as the big black crows I used to see above the fields in New Hampshire. At festival time there is liquor and food, ritual, discipline, and abandonment. There is music and drunkenness and invocation. There is hope. Another season has come. Another season has gone.

I am racially Japanese. I have a certain claim to this crazy place where the prayers intoned by a neighboring Shinto priest (standing in for my grandmother's nephew who is sick) are drowned out by the rehearsals for the pop singing contest in which most of the villagers will compete later that night. The village elders, the priest, and I stand respectfully upon the immaculate, shining wooden floor of the outer shrine, bowing our heads before the hidden powers. During the patchy intervals when I can hear him, I notice the priest has a stutter. His voice flutters up to my ears only occasionally because two men and a woman are singing gustily into a microphone in the compound, testing the sound system. A prerecorded tape of guitars, samisens,[1] and drums accompanies them. Rock music and Shinto prayers. That night, to loud applause and cheers, a young man is given the award for the most *net-suretsu*—passionate, burning—rendition of a song. We roar our approval of the reward. Never mind that his voice had wandered and slid, now slightly above, now slightly below the given line of the melody. Netsuretsu. Netsuretsu.

In the morning, my grandmother's sister kneels at the foot of the stone stairs to offer her morning prayers. She is too crippled to climb the stairs, so each morning she kneels here upon the path. She shuts her eyes for a few seconds, her motions as matter of fact as when she washes rice. I linger longer than she does, so reluctant to leave, savoring the connection I feel with my grandmother in America, the past, and the power that lives and shines in the morning sun.

Our family has served this shrine for generations. The family's need to protect this claim to identity and place outweighs any individual claim to any individual hope. I am Japanese.

---

[1]*samisen:* A guitar-like instrument with a long neck and three strings.

13

I Am a Japanese-American

"Weak." I hear the voice from my childhood years. "Passive," I 9
hear. Our parents and grandparents were the ones who were put into
those camps. They went without resistance; they offered cooperation
as proof of loyalty to America. "Victim," I hear. And, "Silent."

Our parents are painted as hard workers who were socially un- 10
comfortable and had difficulty expressing even the smallest opinion.
Clean, quiet, motivated, and determined to match the American way;
that is us, and that is the story of our time here.

"Why did you go into those camps?" I raged at my parents, fright- 11
ened by my own inner silence and timidity. "Why didn't you do anything to resist? Why didn't you name it the injustice it was?" Couldn't
our parents even think? Couldn't they? Why were we so passive?

I shift my vision and my stance. I am in California. My uncle is 12
in the midst of the sweet potato harvest. He is pressed, trying to get the
harvesting crews onto the field as quickly as possible, worried about the
flow of equipment and people. His big pickup is pulled off to the side,
motor running, door ajar. I see two tractors in the yard in front of an
old shed; the flatbed harvesting platform on which the workers will
stand has already been brought over from the other field. It's early
morning. The workers stand loosely grouped and at ease, but my uncle
looks as harried and tense as a police officer trying to unsnarl a New
York City traffic jam. Driving toward the shed, I pull my car off the road
to make way for an approaching tractor. The front wheels of the car
sink luxuriously into the soft, white sand by the roadside and the car
slides to a dreamy halt, tail still on the road. I try to move forward. I try
to move back. The front bites contentedly into the sand, the back lifts
itself at a jaunty angle. My uncle sees me and storms down the road,
running. He is shouting before he is even near me.

"What's the matter with you?" he screams. "What the hell are you 13
doing?" In his frenzy, he grabs his hat off his head and slashes it through
the air across his knee. He is beside himself. "Don't you know how to
drive in sand? What's the matter with you? You've blocked the whole
roadway. How am I supposed to get my tractors out of here? Can't you
use your head? You've cut off the whole roadway, and we've got to get
out of here."

I stand on the road before him helplessly thinking, "No, I don't 14
know how to drive in sand. I've never driven in sand."

"I'm sorry, uncle," I say, burying a smile beneath a look of sin- 15 cere apology. I notice my deep amusement and my affection for him with great curiosity. I am usually devastated by anger. Not this time.

During the several years that follow I learn about the people and the place, and much more about what has happened in this California village where my parents grew up. The issei, our grandparents, made this settlement in the desert. Their first crops were eaten by rabbits and ravaged by insects. The land was so barren that men walking from house to house sometimes got lost. Women came here too. They bore children in 114-degree heat, then carried the babies with them into the fields to nurse when they reached the end of each row of grapes or other truck-farm crops.

I had had no idea what it meant to buy this kind of land and make it grow green. Or how, when the war came, there was no space at all for the subtlety of being who we were—Japanese-Americans. Either/or was the way. I hadn't understood that people were literally afraid for their lives then, that their money had been frozen in banks; that there was a five-mile travel limit; that when the early evening curfew came and they were inside their houses, some of them watched helplessly as people they knew went into their barns to steal their belongings. The police were patrolling the road, interested only in violators of curfew. There was no help for them in the face of thievery. I had not been able to imagine before what it must have felt like to be an American—to know absolutely that one is an American—and yet to have almost everyone else deny it. Not only deny it, but challenge that identity with machine guns and troops of white American soldiers. In those circumstances it was difficult to say, "I'm a Japanese-American." "American" had to do.

But now I can say that I am a Japanese-American. It means I have a place here in this country, too. I have a place here on the East Coast, where our neighbor is so much a part of our family that my mother never passes her house at night without glancing at the lights to see if she is home and safe; where my parents have hauled hundreds of pounds of rocks from fields and arduously planted Christmas trees and blueberries, lilacs, asparagus, and crab apples; where my father still dreams of angling a stream to a new bed so that he can dig a pond in the field and fill it with water and fish. "The neighbors already came for their Christmas tree?" he asks in December. "Did they like it? Did they like it?"

I have a place on the West Coast where my relatives still farm, where I heard the stories of feuds and backbiting, and where I saw that people survived and flourished because fundamentally they trusted and relied upon one another. A death in the family is not just a death in a family; it is a death in the community. I saw people help each other with money, materials, labor, attention, and time. I saw men gather once a year, without fail, to clean the grounds of a ninety-year-old woman who had helped the community before, during, and after the war. I saw her remembering them with birthday cards sent to each of their children.

I come from a people with a long memory and a distinctive grace. 20 We live our thanks. And we are Americans. Japanese-Americans.

I Am a Japanese-American Woman

Woman. The last piece of my identity. It has been easier by far 21 for me to know myself in Japan and to see my place in America than it has been to accept my line of connection with my own mother. She was my dark self, a figure in whom I thought I saw all that I feared most in myself. Growing into womanhood and looking for some model of strength, I turned away from her. Of course, I could not find what I sought. I was looking for a black feminist or a white feminist. My mother is neither white nor black.

My mother is a woman who speaks with her life as much as with 22 her tongue. I think of her with her own mother. Grandmother had Parkinson's disease and it had frozen her gait and set her fingers, tongue, and feet jerking and trembling in a terrible dance. My aunts and uncles wanted her to be able to live in her own home. They fed her, bathed her, dressed her, awoke at midnight to take her for one last trip to the bathroom. My aunts (her daughters-in-law) did most of the care, but my mother went from New Hampshire to California each summer to spend a month living with Grandmother, because she wanted to and because she wanted to give my aunts at least a small rest. During those hot summer days, mother lay on the couch watching the television or reading, cooking foods that Grandmother liked, and speaking little. Grandmother thrived under her care.

The time finally came when it was too dangerous for Grand- 23 mother to live alone. My relatives kept finding her on the floor beside her bed when they went to wake her in the mornings. My mother flew to California to help clean the house and make arrangements for Grandmother to enter a local nursing home. On her last day at home, while Grandmother was sitting in her big, overstuffed armchair, hair combed and wearing a green summer dress, my mother went to her and knelt at her feet. "Here, Mamma," she said. "I've polished your shoes." She lifted Grandmother's legs and helped her into the shiny black shoes. My

Grandmother looked down and smiled slightly. She left her house walking, supported by her children, carrying her pocketbook, and wearing her polished black shoes. "Look, Mamma," my mom had said, kneeling. "I've polished your shoes."

Just the other day, my mother came to Boston to visit. She had 24 recently lost a lot of weight and was pleased with her new shape and her feeling of good health. "Look at me, Kes," she exclaimed, turning toward me, front and back, as naked as the day she was born. I saw her small breasts and the wide, brown scar, belly button to pubic hair, that marked her because my brother and I were both born by Caesarean section. Her hips were small. I was not a large baby, but there was so little room for me in her that when she was carrying me she could not even begin to bend over toward the floor. She hated it, she said.

"Don't I look good? Don't you think I look good?" 25

I looked at my mother, smiling and as happy as she, thinking of 26 all the times I have seen her naked. I have seen both my parents naked throughout my life, as they have seen me. From childhood through adulthood we've had our naked moments, sharing baths, idle conversations picked up as we moved between showers and closets, hurried moments at the beginning of days, quiet moments at the end of days.

I know this to be Japanese, this ease with the physical, and it 27 makes me think of an old Japanese folk song. A young nursemaid, a fifteen-year-old girl, is singing a lullaby to a baby who is strapped to her back. The nursemaid has been sent as a servant to a place far from her own home. "We're the beggars," she says, "and they are the nice people. Nice people wear fine sashes. Nice clothes."

If I should drop dead, 28
bury me by the roadside!
I'll give a flower
to everyone who passes.

What kind of flower? 29
The cam-cam-camellia [tsun-tsun-tsubaki]
watered by Heaven:
alms water.

The nursemaid is the intersection of heaven and earth, the inter- 30 section of the human, the natural world, the body, and the soul. In this song, with clear eyes, she looks steadily at life, which is sometimes so very terrible and sad. I think of her while looking at my mother, who is standing on the red and purple carpet before me, laughing, without any clothes.

I am my mother's daughter. And I am myself.   31
I am a Japanese-American woman.   32

EPILOGUE

I recently heard a man from West Africa share some memories   33
of his childhood. He was raised Muslim, but when he was a young man, he found himself deeply drawn to Christianity. He struggled against his inner impulse for years, trying to avoid the church yet feeling pushed to return to it again and again. "I would have done *anything* to avoid the change," he said. At last, he became Christian. Afterwards he was afraid to go home, fearing that he would not be accepted. The fear was groundless, he discovered, when at last he returned—he had separated himself, but his family and friends (all Muslim) had not separated themselves from him.

The man, who is now a professor of religion, said that in the Africa   34
he knew as a child and a young man, pluralism was embraced rather than feared. There was "a kind of tolerance that did not deny your particularity," he said. He alluded to zestful, spontaneous debates that would sometimes loudly erupt between Muslims and Christians in the village's public spaces. His memories of an atheist who harangued the villagers when he came to visit them once a week moved me deeply. Perhaps the man was an agricultural advisor or inspector. He harassed the women. He would say: "Don't go to the fields! Don't even bother to go to the fields. Let God take care of you. He'll send you the food. If you believe in God, why do you need to work? You don't need to work! Let God put the seeds in the ground. Stay home."

The professor said, "The women laughed, you know? They just   35
laughed. Their attitude was, 'Here is a child of God. When will he come home?' "

The storyteller, the professor of religion, smiled a most fantastic   36
tender smile as he told this story. "In my country, there is a deep affirmation of the oneness of God," he said. "The atheist and the women were having quite different experiences in their encounter, though the atheist did not know this. He saw himself as quite separate from the women. But the women did not see themselves as being separate from him. 'Here is a child of God,' they said. 'When will he come home?' "

THE PRISM OF
SELF-IMAGE

Ellyn Kaschak

■

GENDER STEREOTYPING IN CONTEMPORARY AMERICAN *culture is the focus of this brief excerpt from* Engendered Lives: A New Psychology of Women's Experience *(1992).* Engendered Lives *won the Critics Choice Award of the American Educational Studies Association. It was written by Ellyn Kaschak, a psychology professor and professional therapist who has served as chair of the Marriage, Family, and Child Counseling Program at San Jose State University.*

In "The Prism of Self-Image," Kaschak argues that the sense of who you are as a woman or as a man is less a matter of nature than nurture. According to this view, gender identity is "socially constructed," meaning that from the day we are born, we are bombarded with messages about what it means to be a girl or boy in our society. These messages tell us what to wear, how to walk, when to speak, and what to say. Most important, they tell us what we are worth. We are promised that if we live up to expectations, we will be rewarded with love and approval.

The primary message girls get as they grow up, according to Kaschak, is that appearance is everything. If they want to be loved, they must make themselves attractive to men. She explains that this message is broadcast early and often through the media. Kaschak briefly looks at three aspects of contemporary culture in which girls see themselves reflected: television, toys, and magazines. As you read, try to think of examples either to support or contradict Kaschak's argument. You might assume that Kaschak's argument is dated because it is based on research from the 1980s, but consider this: in 1996, the Barbie doll was the number one best-selling toy for girls.

In the room of mirrors, girls stand in front of each mirror and practice smiling, practice widening their eyes, practice cocking an eyebrow, practice walking, practice moving. They must practice until their movements achieve spontaneity. . . . They are invisible to each other, invisible to themselves.

—Gabrielle Burton
Heartbreak Hotel

To be a woman means to live one's life in a mirror world, but not the kind of mirrors of which we ordinarily speak. Perhaps a prism would serve as a more apt metaphor, dividing women, like so many frequencies of light, into their component parts. Refracted back are only those parts and qualities that masculine society and individual men deem important, those by which they evaluate attractiveness and femininity. Women's images are refracted back to them evaluated or contextualized, that is, distorted. Some parts of the various and complex aspects of themselves are fragmented, others are completely invisible. In the mirror, a woman sees how she deviates from the ideal in her size, shape, race, or age. . . .

The most common mirror of all in modern society is the television set. It is also, in fact, the most frequently used baby-sitter. Even in families in which the mother does not work outside the home, children spend the greatest proportion of their time not with her but with the TV set. And television, especially commercial advertising, is a primary source of gender stereotyping and of the emphasis on physical attractiveness for females. Billions of dollars are spent every year on advertising cosmetics, physical fitness, and weight reduction (Berscheid and Walster 1984). A. Chris Downs and Sheila K. Harrison (1985) found that the highest proportion of beauty and weight messages were found in food and drink commercials, followed by personal care and household product messages, and then by clothing advertisements. They estimate that children and adult television viewers are confronted with over 5,200 attractiveness messages per year, 1,850 of which deal directly with (female) beauty—virtually all implicitly. The greatest proportion of attractiveness messages consist of female performers with male announcers, the epitome of the indeterminate observer.

A study of the ten most popular children's TV shows revealed that four had no female characters at all. The other six were predominantly male, with females as witches or magical creatures or in deferential roles. Even on "Sesame Street," the most popular educational show for children, not one of the primary monster characters is female. Similarly, popular children's stories show girls and women primarily in observer roles and almost always wearing aprons—even the female animals (Romer 1981).

In Western society, toys also play a major part in socializing and mirroring for children how and in what qualities they should be investing themselves. They are as important as television in physically based gender learning. For one thing, they induce separateness and separate play. They serve most often as a substitute for interpersonal relatedness and, as such, are socially constructed transitional objects. It has recently been reported, in this regard, that girls' toys, more than ever, involve play with hair and makeup. It has been noted that girls' toys, even today, focus on appearance, makeup, dating fantasies, and dressing up dolls, especially Barbie dolls. In addition, there are new games that encourage girls not yet in their teens to compete for the date of their dreams. " 'Girls' play involves dressing and grooming and acting out their future—going on a date, getting married—and boys' play involves competition and conflict, good guys and bad guys,' said Glenn Bozarth, director of public relations for Mattel, which makes the Barbie doll" (Lawson, 1989). Many parents say that it is impossible to buck the tide of toys for girls that involve passive play and looks, and for boys that involve active and aggressive learning. One parent is quoted as saying: "I wanted my kids to be raised with a higher degree of consciousness, but you can't force it. . . . I tried to get my daughter to play with GI Joe and my son with dolls. It didn't work. My daughter's favorite toy is Barbie. I am aghast" (p. 5L).

He would also be aghast to discover that there are even more appearance-related toys for girls these days. Toy manufacturers such as Mattel make stick-on painted fingernails for little girls, along with eye shadow, blusher, and lipstick. Maybelline has introduced a bubble gum–flavored lip gloss. A popular doll by Mattel is Li'l Miss Make-up, who resembles a little girl. When brushed with cold water, she develops eyebrows, colored eyelids and fingernails, and tinted lips (Wells 1989). Many of the girls who play with this kind of doll will grow up to read women's magazines and watch soap operas—that is, to be properly socialized as women.

An informal survey of magazines for adolescent girls turned up an emphasis on clothing, makeup, appearance, and how to "get guys." The emphasis was on appearance, appearance, appearance. Several contained articles by males giving advice to females or even ridiculing them, like one from *Seventeen* that explained: "in high school girls . . .

21

appear to be getting a better sense of what they actually want to do with their lives. And, to put it bluntly, it has a dulling effect on their personalities" (Schaefers 1989, p. 68). The more mature woman can read in *Mademoiselle* (August 1989) of the power of the orgasm to increase the beauty of her physical appearance or else can take more mundane paths such as fashion and makeup. The New Woman who reads the magazine of the same name considers career and finances along with beauty, appearance, and how to win and keep her man.

Turning to men's magazines, we start in adolescence with cars and women's bodies *(Playboy)* and move on to *Esquire* and its ilk, which, for example, in August 1989 contained an article called "Women We Love and Women We Don't," the latter being ridiculed for physical appearance, obesity, and the like, as much as the former were admired/desired for their beauty. No articles or ads appeared on how to lose weight, how to attract women, how to have more satisfying sex, and certainly not on how to improve physical appearance. Nothing was said about the glow of beauty induced by orgasm. 7

With all of these socially constructed imperatives, what woman can accurately perceive herself in a mirror? Self-esteem becomes self-image, and women's images are always found wanting. Some body part is inevitably too big, too small, or the wrong shape. In a study reported by Russell Belk, "women saw their bodies — particularly external parts such as eyes, hair, legs and skin — as more central to their identities than men did to theirs" (1988, p. 52). Of course they would, since they *are*, in a much more essential way, their bodies. Here again it is precisely those body parts, and only those, that are considered worth looking at with which these women identified themselves. The male perspective is incorporated into the female identity. 8

References

Belk, R. W. 1988. My possessions myself. *Psychology Today* (July): 51–52.

Berscheid, E., and E. Walster. 1984. Physical attractiveness. In *Advances in Experimental Social Psychology*. Edited by L. Berkowitz. New York: Academic Press.

Burton, G. 1988. *Heartbreak Hotel*. New York: Penguin Books.

Downs, A. C., and S. K. Harrison. 1985. Embarrassing age spots or just plain ugly? Physical attractiveness stereotyping as an instrument of sexism on American television commercials. *Sex Roles* 13(1/2):9–19.

Lawson, C. 1989. In age of feminism, girls' toys are still sugar and spice. *San Jose Mercury News,* June 25, p. 5L.

Romer, N. 1981. *The Sex-Role Cycle: Socialization from Infancy to Old Age.* New York: McGraw-Hill.

Schaefers, J. 1989. *Seventeen* magazine (July): 68.

Wells, L. 1989. *New York Times Magazine.* Cited in *On the Issues* 12:6.

BARBIE DOLL

Marge Piercy

∎

ALTHOUGH "BARBIE DOLL" WAS WRITTEN in 1973, many years before Ellyn Kaschak wrote Engendered Lives, *it is an illustration of Kaschak's argument that for girls in our society: "Self-esteem becomes self-image, and women's images are always found wanting. Some body part is inevitably too big, too small, or the wrong shape."*

Marge Piercy is a prolific writer who has written more than two dozen books of poetry. Most of her novels and poems, like "Barbie Doll," are explicitly feminist. Many readers, especially women who grew up with Barbie, find the poem enormously powerful because it reminds them of women who will do anything—from dieting to plastic surgery—to achieve an ideal self. Other readers who mistakenly equate feminism with hatred of men, however, dismiss the poem as a feminist tract. They think "Barbie Doll" blames men rather than the culture in general for the negative image many women have of themselves. As you read the poem, think about Kaschak's cultural analysis and consider what you think Piercy is saying in "Barbie Doll."

This girlchild was born as usual
and presented dolls that did pee-pee
and miniature GE stoves and irons
and wee lipsticks the color of cherry candy.
Then in the magic of puberty, a classmate said: 5
You have a great big nose and fat legs.

She was healthy, tested intelligent,
possessed strong arms and back,

24

abundant sexual drive and manual dexterity.
She went to and fro apologizing. 10
Everyone saw a fat nose on thick legs.

She was advised to play coy,
exhorted to come on hearty,
exercise, diet, smile and wheedle.
Her good nature wore out 15
like a fan belt.
So she cut off her nose and her legs
and offered them up.

In the casket displayed on satin she lay
with the undertaker's cosmetics painted on, 20
a turned-up putty nose,
dressed in a pink and white nightie.
Doesn't she look pretty? everyone said.
Consummation at last.
To every woman a happy ending. 25

DREAMING OF HEROES

H. G. Bissinger

■

In Ellyn Kaschak's essay and Marge Piercy's poem, you read about the impact of stereotyping on women's sense of identity. In this selection by journalist H. G. Bissinger, you will read about men and how their ideas of identity and self-worth are formed. "Dreaming of Heroes" originally appeared in Friday Night Lights: A Town, a Team, and a Dream *(1990), a profile of the town of Odessa, Texas, and its inhabitants. Bissinger, a Pulitzer Prize–winning reporter, was on the staff of the* Philadelphia Inquirer *for seven years.*

As you read, recall what Kaschak said about boys learning from their toys and games to be active and aggressive. Also remember Kaschak quoting the Mattel toy company director of public relations who asserts that "boys' play involves competition and conflict, good guys and bad guys." Activity, aggressiveness, competition, and conflict are all part of the sports played by Mike Winchell, one of the main characters in Bissinger's book, but as you read consider whether they are the qualities Mike learns to value most highly in himself. Consider also how Mike acquires his self-image, specifically whether he sees himself mirrored in other people's eyes, like the girls Kaschak describes.

When his father gazed at him from the hospital bed with   1
those sad eyes that had drawn so narrow from the drinking and the
smoking and the endless heartache, Mike Winchell had been thirteen
years old. He knew something was wrong because of the way his father
acted with him, peaceful in the knowledge he didn't have to put up a
fight anymore. Mike tried to joke with him as he always had, but Billy

Winchell didn't have time for playful banter. He was serious now, and he wanted Mike to listen.

He brought up Little League and warned Mike that the pitchers 2 were going to get better now and the home runs wouldn't come as easily as they once had. He told him he had to go to college, there could be no two ways about it. He let him know it was okay to have a little beer every now and then because the Winchells were, after all, German, and Germans loved their beer, but he admonished him to never, ever try drugs. And he told his son he loved him.

He didn't say much more after that, the arthritis eating into his 3 hips and the agony of the oil field accident that had cost him his leg too much for him now. In the early morning silence of that hospital room in Odessa, he let go.

Mike ran out of the room when it happened, wanting to be by himself, to get as far away as he possibly could, and his older brother, Joe 4 Bill, made no attempt to stop him. He knew Mike would be back because he had always been that kind of kid, quiet, loyal, unfailingly steady. Mike didn't go very far. He stopped in front of the fountain at the hospital entrance and sat by himself. It was one in the morning and hardly anything stirred in those wide downtown streets. He cried a little but he knew he would be all right because, ever since the split-up of his parents when he was five, he had pretty much raised himself. Typically, he didn't worry about himself. He worried about his grandmother.

But he didn't want to stay in Odessa anymore. It was too ugly for 5 him and the land itself bore no secrets nor ever inspired the imagination, so damn flat, as he later put it, that a car ran down the highway and never disappeared. He longed for lakes and trees and hills, for serene places where he could take walks by himself.

Mike came back to the hospital after about half an hour. "You 6 were the most special thing in his life," his brother told him. "It's a hard pill to swallow, but you're gonna have to make him proud of you." As for leaving Odessa to come live with him, Joe Bill gently talked Mike out of it. He used the most powerful pull there was for a thirteen-year-old boy living in Odessa, really the only one that gave a kid something to dream about—the power of Permian football.

He talked about how Mike had always wanted to wear the black 7 and white and how much he would regret it if he didn't because there were so few places that could offer the same sense of allegiance and tradition. Mike knew that Joe Bill was right. He had already carried that dream for a long time, and despite what he thought of Odessa, it was impossible to let it go.

He stayed in Odessa and sometimes, when he went over to his 8
grandmother's house and talked about his father, it helped him through
the pain of knowing that Billy was gone forever. "His daddy worshiped
him," said Julia Winchell. "He sure loved that little boy." And Mike returned that love.

"When he died, I just thought that the best person in the world 9
had just died."

Billy and Mike.
There was Mike, smiling, curly-haired, looking into his dad's face 10
at Christmastime. And there was Billy, thin and wizened and slightly
hunched, like a walking stick that had warped in the rain. There was
Mike at the flea markets they went to together on Saturdays and Sun-
days over on University, helping his father lift the boxes from the car
and set them in the little booth. There was Billy following him to a chair
so he could sit and rest. There they were together on those hot after-
noons that Mike hated so much but never complained about, selling the
cheap tools and knives and toys and Spanish Bibles that had been found
in catalogues or on trips to Mexico.

There was Mike playing Little League baseball with that go-to- 11
hell stance of his—feet close together, up on the toes, taking as big a
stride as he could possibly muster into the ball—jacking one homer
after another. And there was Billy, the proud master, watching his
gifted disciple from the car, unable to get out because of the pain in his
leg and the arthritis.

Under the demanding tutelage of his father, Mike could do no 12
wrong in Little League. He became the stuff of legend, with twenty-
seven pitches in a row thrown for strikes, a single season in which he
hit thirty home runs. And then somewhere around the time his father
started slipping, Mike lost that innate confidence in himself. The gift
was always there, but he began to question it, doubt it, brood over it.
When he hit three homers in a game once, he didn't go back to the
bench feeling exalted. "Why in the hell can I hit these home runs?" he
asked himself. "Why could I do it when other kids couldn't?"

There had always been something inward and painfully shy about 13
Mike, but the death of his father forced him to grow up even faster than
he already had. He knew Billy was in pain and he also knew that only
death could stop it. "It was hurtin' 'im and there was nothin' they could
do," he said. "You don't want nobody to die, but you don't want him
hurtin' all the time either."

After Billy died, Mike's life didn't get any easier. He had a brother 14 who was sent to prison for stealing. At home he lived with his mother, who worked at a service station convenience store as a clerk. They didn't have much money. His mother was enormously quiet and reserved, almost like a phantom. Coach Gaines, who spent almost as much time dealing with parents as he did with the players, had never met her.

Mike himself almost never talked of his mother, and he was reluctant to let people into his home, apparently because of its condition. "He never wants me to come in," said his girlfriend, DeAnn. "He never wants me to be inside, ever." When they got together it was over at his grandmother's, and that's where his yard sign was, announcing to the world that he was a Permian football player.

"Me and him talked about not havin' a nice home or a nice car and how those things were not important," said Joe Bill. "I told him, you make your grades and stay in sports, you'll one day have those things."

Mike persevered, a coach's dream who worked hard and became a gifted student of the game of football, just as he had in baseball with his father. The one ceaseless complaint was that he thought too much, and he knew that was true, that whenever he threw the ball he didn't just wing it, go with his instincts, but sometimes seemed to agonize over it, a checklist racing through his mind even as he backpedaled—*be careful . . . get the right touch now . . . watch the wrist, watch the wrist! . . . don't overthrow it now, don't throw an interception. . . .*

He started at quarterback his junior year at Permian, but his own obvious lack of confidence caused some of his teammates to lose faith in him in a tight game. When the pressure was off and the score wasn't close, it was hard to find a better quarterback. When the pressure was on, though, something seemed to unravel inside him. But now he was a senior and had had a whole year to process the incredible feeling of walking into a stadium and seeing twenty thousand fans expecting the world from him. He seemed ready, ready for something truly wonderful to happen to him.

He didn't dwell much on his father's death anymore. It had been four years since it happened and Mike had moved on since then. But he still thought about him from time to time, and he said he had never met anyone more honest, or more clever, or more dependable. He smiled as he talked about what a good "horse trader" Billy was, and how he loved animals, and how he had bought him every piece of sports equipment that had ever been invented. When he had had trouble with his baseball swing, he knew that Billy would have been able to fix it in a second, standing with him, showing him where to place his hands, jiggering his stance just a tad here and a tad there, doing all the things only a dad could do to make a swing level again and keep a baseball flying forever.

And Mike also knew how much Billy Winchell would have cherished seeing him on this September night, dressed in the immaculate black and white of the Permian Panthers, moments away from playing out the dream that had kept him in Odessa. The two-a-days in the August heat were over now. The Watermelon Feed had come and gone, and so had the pre-season scrimmage. Now came the Friday night lights. Now it was showtime and the first game of the season.

Most everyone thought that Billy Winchell had given up on himself by the time he died. But they also knew that if there was anything making him hold on, it was Mike.

Billy and Mike.

"He would have liked to have lived for Mike's sake," said Julia Winchell. "He sure would have been proud of him."

"Some of you haven't played before, been in the spotlight," said assistant coach Tam Hollingshead in those waning hours before Permian would take the field against El Paso Austin. He knew what the jitters of the season opener could do, how the most talented kid could come unglued in the sea of all those lights and those thousands of fans. He offered some succinct advice.

"Have some fun, hustle your ass, and stick the hell out of 'em."

"It's not a party we're goin' to, it's a business trip," Mike Belew told the running backs. "If you get hurt, that's fine, you're hurt. But if you get a lick, and you're gonna lay there and whine about it, you don't belong on the field anyway."

The team left the field house and made its way to the stadium in a caravan of yellow school buses. They went through their pre-game warmups with methodical, meticulous determination. Then they went to the dressing room and sat in silence before Gaines called the team to huddle around him. He didn't say much. He didn't have to.

Everyone knew what was at stake, that if all went without a hitch, this game would be the beginning of a glorious stretch that would not end until the afternoon of December 17 with a state championship trophy. It would be a sixteen-game season, longer than that of any college team in America and as long as most of the pro teams' seasons. Three and a half months of pure devotion to football where nothing else mattered, nothing else made a difference.

"That 1988 season is four and a half minutes away," Gaines said 29
quietly with a little smile still on his lips. "Let's have a great one."

At the very sight of the team at the edge of the stadium, hundreds 30
of elementary school kids started squealing in delight. They wore imitation cheerleading costumes and sweatshirts that said PERMIAN PANTHERS #1. They began yelling the war cry of "*MO-JO! MO-JO! MO-JO!*" in frantic unison, rocking their arms back and forth. A little girl in glasses put her hand to her mouth, as if she had seen something incredible, and it made her momentarily speechless between screams. As the black wave of the Permian players moved out into the middle of the field, eight thousand other souls who had filled the home side rose to give a standing ovation. This moment, and not January first, was New Year's day.

Brian Johnson opened the season with a fifteen-yard run off the 31
right side through a gaping hole to the Permian 47, lurching forward for every possible extra inch. Two quick passes from Winchell to split end Lloyd Hill gave Permian a first down at the El Paso Austin ten. Winchell looked good, setting up with poise in the pocket, throwing nicely, no rushed throws skittering off the hand.

Then Don Billingsley, the starting tailback for the Permian Pan- 32
thers, got the ball on a pitch. He was a senior, and it was his debut as a starter.

The roars of the crowd got louder and louder as Don took the 33
ball and headed for the goal line. A touchdown on the first drive of the season seemed destined, to the delight of the thousands who were there. And no one wanted it more, no one felt it more, than Charlie Billingsley.

It was his son Don down there on that field with the ball. But it 34
was more than the natural swell of parental pride that stirred inside him.

Twenty years earlier, Charlie Billingsley himself had worn the 35
black and white of Permian, not as some two-bit supporter but as a star, a legend. He still had powerful memories of those days, and as he sat in the stands on this balmy and beautiful night where the last wisps of clouds ran across the sky like a residue of ash from a once-brilliant fire, it seemed impossible not to look down on the field and see his own reflection.

LARGER THAN LIFE

Jenny Lyn Bader

■

"LARGER THAN LIFE" CONSTRASTS SHARPLY with "Dreaming of Heroes." Whereas H. G. Bissinger describes a community that continues to dream of and inspire heroes, Jenny Lyn Bader describes a generation that has lost its faith in heroes. Bader, a playwright and essayist, wrote this piece originally for an anthology called Next: Young American Writers on the New Generation *(1994). In it, she speaks not only for herself but also for her generation when she claims that the heroic age has passed.*

Bader explains that as a child growing up in the seventies, she was an enthusiastic hero worshipper who dutifully admired all the usual suspects such as Abraham Lincoln and Eleanor Roosevelt. But by then, heroism was already on the decline. Bader speculates about some possible causes for the decline.

She also suggests that, for many of her contemporaries, role models have taken the place of heroes. The distinctions she draws between heroes and role models are insightful and amusing. For example, she explains that while heroes are "visionaries" who inspire us, role models "have a job, accomplishment, or hairstyle worth emulating."

You'll find a lot to think about as you read this essay. You may, for example, question whether young people today really have given up heroes and replaced them with role models. You might also want to take an informal poll to see how many of the people Bader mentions in the essay are regarded as heroes and, if so, determine why they are.

When my grandmother was young, she would sometimes spot the emperor Franz Josef riding down the cobbled roads of the Austro-Hungarian Empire.

She came of age so long ago that the few surviving photographs   2
are colored cream and chestnut. Early on, she saw cars replace horses
and carriages. When she got older, she marveled at the first televisions.
Near the end of her life, she grew accustomed to remote control and
could spot prime ministers on color TV. By the time she died, the
world was freshly populated by gadgetry and myth. Her generation
bore witness to the rise of new machinery created by visionaries. My
generation has seen machinery break down and visionaries come under
fire.

As children, we enjoyed collecting visionaries, the way we col-   3
lected toys or baseball cards. When I was a kid, I first met Patrick
Henry and Eleanor Roosevelt, Abraham Lincoln and Albert Einstein.
They could always be summoned by the imagination and so were never
late for play dates. I thought heroes figured in any decent childhood. I
knew their stats.

Nathan Hale. Nelson Mandela. Heroes have guts.   4

Michelangelo. Shakespeare. Heroes have imagination.   5

They fight. Alexander the Great. Joan of Arc.   6

They fight for what they believe in. Susan B. Anthony. Martin   7
Luther King.

Heroes overcome massive obstacles. Beethoven, while deaf, still   8
managed to carry an unforgettable tune. Homer, while blind, never
failed to give an excellent description. Helen Keller, both deaf and
blind, still spoke to the world. FDR, despite his polio, became president. Moses, despite his speech impediment, held productive discus-
sions with God.

They inspire three-hour movies. They make us weepy. They do   9
the right thing while enduring attractive amounts of suffering. They
tend to be self-employed. They are often killed off. They sense the future. They lead lives that make us question our own. They are our ideals,
but not our friends.

They don't have to be real. Some of them live in books and leg-   10
ends. They don't have to be famous. There are lower-profile heroes
who get resurrected by ambitious biographers. There are collective heroes: firefighters and astronauts, unsung homemakers, persecuted peoples. There are those whose names we can't remember, only their
deeds: "you know, that woman who swam the English Channel," "the
guy who died running the first marathon," "the student who threw himself in front of the tank at Tiananmen Square." There are those whose
names we'll never find out: the anonymous benefactor, the masked
man, the undercover agent, the inventor of the wheel, the unknown sol-

dier. The one who did the thing so gutsy and terrific that no one will ever know what it was.

Unlike icons (Marilyn, Elvis) heroes are not only sexy but noble, too. Unlike idols (Gretzky, Streisand), who vary from fan to fan, they are almost universally beloved. Unlike icons and idols, heroes lack irony. And unlike icons and idols, heroes are no longer in style. 11

As centuries end, so do visions of faith—maybe because the faithful get nervous as the double zeroes approach and question what they've been worshiping. Kings and queens got roughed up at the end of the eighteenth century; God took a beating at the end of the nineteenth; and as the twentieth century draws to a close, outstanding human beings are the casualties of the moment. In the 1970s and 1980s, Americans started feeling queasy about heroism. Those of us born in the sixties found ourselves on the cusp of that change. A sweep of new beliefs, priorities, and headlines has conspired to take our pantheon away from us. 12

Members of my generation believed in heroes when they were younger but now find themselves grasping for them. Even the word *hero* sounds awkward. I find myself embarrassed to ask people who their heroes are, because the word just doesn't trip off the tongue. My friend Katrin sounded irritated when I asked for hers. She said, "Oh, Jesus . . . Do people still have heroes?" 13

We don't. Certainly not in the traditional sense of adoring perfect people. Frequently not at all. "I'm sort of intrigued by the fact that I don't have heroes right off the top of my head," said a colleague, Peter. "Can I get back to you?" 14

Some of us are more upset about this than others. It's easy to tell which of us miss the heroic age. We are moved by schmaltzy political speeches, we warm up to stories of pets saving their owners, we even get misty-eyed watching the Olympics. We mope when model citizens fail us. My college roommate, Linda, remembers a seventh-grade class called "Heroes and She-roes." The first assignment was to write about a personal hero or she-ro. "I came home," Linda told me, "and cried and cried because I didn't have one. . . . Carter had screwed up in Iran and given the malaise speech. Gerald Ford was a nothing and Nixon was evil. My parents told me to write about Jane Fonda the political activist and I just kept crying." 15

Not everyone feels sentimental about it. A twentyish émigré raised in the former Soviet Union told me: "It's kind of anticlimactic to look for heroes when you've been brought up in a culture that insists on so many heroes. . . . What do you want me to say? Lenin? Trotsky?" Even 16 though I grew up in the relatively propaganda-free United States, I understood. The America of my childhood insisted on heroes, too.

Of all the myths I happily ate for breakfast, the most powerful one   17
was our story of revolution. I sang about it as early as kindergarten and read about it long after. The story goes, a few guys in wigs skipped town on some grumpy church leaders and spurned a loopy king to branch out on their own. The children who hear the story realize they don't have to believe in oldfangled clergy or a rusty crown—but they had better believe in those guys with the wigs.

I sure did. I loved a set of books known as the "Meet" series: *Meet*   18
George Washington, Meet Andrew Jackson, Meet the Men Who Sailed the Seas, and many more. I remember one picture of an inspired Thomas Jefferson, his auburn ponytail tied in a black ribbon, penning words with a feather as a battle of banners and cannon fire raged behind him.

A favorite "Meet" book starred Christopher Columbus. His re-   19
sistance to the flat-earth society of his day was engrossing, especially to a kid like me who had trouble trying new foods let alone seeking new land masses. I identified with his yearning for a new world and his difficulty with finding investors. Standing up to the king and queen of Spain was like convincing your parents to let you do stuff they thought was idiotic. Now, my allowance was only thirty-five cents a week, but that didn't mean I wasn't going to ask for three ships at some later date.

This is pretty embarrassing: I adored those guys. The ones in the   20
white powder and ponytails, the voluptuous hats, the little breeches and cuffs. They were funny-looking, but lovable. They did outrageous things without asking for permission. They invented the pursuit of happiness.

I had a special fondness for Ben Franklin, statesman and eccen-   21
tric inventor. Inventions, like heroes, made me feel as though I lived in a dull era. If I'd grown up at the end of the nineteenth century, I could have spoken on early telephones. A few decades later, I could have heard the new sounds of radio. In the sixties, I could have watched black-and-white TVs graduate to color.

Instead, I saw my colorful heroes demoted to black and white.   22
Mostly white. By the time I finished high school, it was no longer hip to look up to the paternalistic dead white males who launched our country, kept slaves and mistresses, and massacred native peoples. Suddenly they weren't visionaries but oppressors, or worse—objects. Samuel Adams became a beer, John Hancock became a building, and the rest of the guys in wigs were knocked off one by one, in a whodunit that couldn't be explained away by the fact of growing up.

The flag-waving of my youth, epitomized by America's bicen- 23
tennial, was a more loving homage than I know today. The year 1976
rolled in while Washington was still reeling from Saigon, but the irony
was lost on me and my second-grade classmates. The idea of losing
seemed miles away. We celebrated July fourth with wide eyes and patriotic parties. Grown-ups had yet to tell themselves (so why should they
tell us?) that the young nation on its birthday had suffered a tragic
defeat.

Historians soon filled us in about that loss, and of others. Dis- 24
covering America was nothing compared to discovering the flaws of its
discoverers, now cast as imperialist sleaze, racist and sexist and genoci-
dal. All things heroic—human potential, spiritual fervor, moral re-
splendence—soon became suspect. With the possible exception of
bodybuilding, epic qualities went out of fashion. Some will remember
1992 as the year Superman died. Literally, the writers and illustrators
at *D.C. Comics* decided the guy was too old to keep leaping buildings
and rescuing an aging damsel in distress. When rumors circulated that
he would be resurrected, readers protested via calls to radio shows, letters to editors, and complaints to stores that they were in no mood for
such an event.

A monster named Doomsday killed Superman, overcoming him 25
not with Kryptonite but with brute force. Who killed the others? I
blame improved modes of character assassination, media hype artists,
and scholars. The experts told me that Columbus had destroyed cultures and ravaged the environment. They also broke the news that the
cowboys had brazenly taken land that wasn't theirs. In a way, I'm glad
I didn't know that earlier; dressing up as a cowgirl for Halloween
wouldn't have felt right. In a more urgent way, I wish I had known it
then so I wouldn't have had to learn it later.

Just fifteen years after America's bicentennial came Columbus's 26
quincentennial, when several towns canceled their annual parades in
protest of his sins. Soon other festivities started to feel funny. When
my aunt served corn pudding last Thanksgiving, my cousin took a
spoonful, then said drily that the dish was made in honor of the Indians who taught us to use corn before we eliminated them. Uncomfort-
able chuckles followed. Actually, neither "we" nor my personal ancestors had come to America in time to kill any Native Americans. Yet the
holiday put us in the same boat with the pilgrims and anchored us in
the white man's domain.

I am fascinated by how we become "we" and "they." It's as if sid- 27
ing with the establishment is the Alka-Seltzer that helps us stomach the

past. To swallow history lessons, we turn into "we": one nation under God of proud but remorseful Indian killers. We also identify with people who look like us. For example, white northerners studying the Civil War identify both with white slaveholders and with northern abolitionists, aligning with both race and place. Transsexuals empathize with men and women. Immigrants identify with their homeland and their adopted country. Historians proposing a black Athena and a black Jesus have inspired more of such bonding.

I'll admit that these empathies can be empowering. I always understood the idea of feeling stranded by unlikely role models but never emotionally grasped it until I watched Penny Marshall's movie *A League of Their Own*. For the first time, I appreciated why so many women complain that sports bore them. I had enjoyed baseball before but never as intensely as I enjoyed the games in that film. The players were people like me. Lori Petty, petite, chirpy, wearing a skirt, commanded the pitcher's mound with such aplomb that I was moved. There's something to be said for identifying with people who remind us of ourselves, though Thomas Jefferson and Lori Petty look more like each other than either of them looks like me. I'll never know if I would've read the "Meet" books with more zeal if they'd described our founding mothers. I liked them as they were.

Despite the thrill of dames batting something on the big screen besides their eyelashes, the fixation on look-alike idols is disturbing for those who get left out. In the movie *White Men Can't Jump*, Wesley Snipes tells Woody Harrelson not to listen to Jimi Hendrix, because "White people can't hear Jimi." Does this joke imply that black people can't hear Mozart? That I can admire Geena Davis's batting but never appreciate Carlton Fisk? Besides dividing us from one another, these emotional allegiances divide us from potential heroes too, causing us to empathize with, say, General Custer and his last stand instead of with Sitting Bull and the victorious Sioux.

Rejecting heroes for having the wrong ethnic credentials or sex organs says less about our multicultural vision than our lack of imagination. By focusing on what we are instead of who we can become, by typecasting and miscasting our ideals—that's how we become "we" and "they." If heroes are those we'd like to emulate, it does make sense that they resemble us. But the focus on physical resemblance seems limited and racist.

Heroes should be judged on their deeds, and there are those with plenty in common heroically but not much in terms of ethnicity, nationality, or gender. Just look at Harriet Tubman and Moses; George

Washington and Simón Bolívar; Mahatma Gandhi and Martin Luther King; Murasaki and Milton; Cicero and Ann Richards. Real paragons transcend nationality. It didn't matter to me that Robin Hood was English—as long as he did good, he was as American as a barbecue. It didn't matter to Queen Isabella that Columbus was Italian as long as he sailed for Spain and sprinkled her flags about. The British epic warrior Beowulf was actually Swedish. Both the German hero Etzel and the Scandinavian hero Atli were really Attila, king of the Huns. With all this borrowing going on, we shouldn't have to check the passports of our luminaries; the idea that we can be like them not literally but spiritually is what's uplifting in the first place.

The idea that we can never be like them has led to what I call jealousy journalism. You know, we're not remotely heroic so let's tear down anyone who is. It's become hard to remember which papers are tabloids. Tell-all articles promise us the "real story"—implying that greatness can't be real. The safe thing about *Meet George Washington* was that you couldn't actually meet him. Today's stories and pictures bring us closer. And actually meeting your heroes isn't the best idea. Who wants to learn that a favorite saint is really just an egomaniac with a publicist? 32

Media maestros have not only knocked public figures off their pedestals, they've also lowered heroism standards by idealizing just about everyone. Oprah, Geraldo, and the rest turn their guests into heroes of the afternoon because they overcame abusive roommates, childhood disfigurement, deranged spouses, multiple genitalia, cheerleading practice, or zany sexual predilections. In under an hour, a studio audience can hear their epic sagas told. 33

While TV and magazine producers helped lead heroes to their graves, the academic community gave the final push. Just as my peers and I made our way through college, curriculum reformers were promoting "P.C." agendas at the expense of humanistic absolutes. Scholars invented their own tabloidism, investigating and maligning both dead professors and trusty historical figures. Even literary theory helped, when deconstructionists made it trendy to look for questions instead of answers, for circular logic instead of linear sense, for defects, contradictions, and the ironic instead of meaning, absolutes, and the heroic. 34

It was the generations that preceded ours who killed off our heroes. And like everyone who crucified a superstar, these people thought they were doing a good thing. The professors and journalists consciously moved in a positive direction—toward greater tolerance, open- 35 ness, and realism—eliminating our inspirations in the process. The death of an era of hero worship was not the result of the cynical, clinical materialism too often identified with my generation. It was the side effect of a complicated cultural surgery, of an operation that may have been necessary and that many prescribed.

So with the best of intentions, these storytellers destroyed bedtime stories. Which is too bad for the kids, because stories make great teachers. Children glean by example. You can't tell a child "Be ingenious," or "Do productive things." You can tell them, "This Paul Revere person jumped on a horse at midnight, rode wildly through the dark, figured out where the mean British troops were coming to attack the warm, fuzzy, sweet, great-looking colonists, and sent messages by code, igniting our fight for freedom," and they'll get the idea. America's rugged values come gift wrapped in the frontier tales of Paul Bunyan, Daniel Boone, Davy Crockett—fables of independence and natural resources. Kids understand that Johnny Appleseed or Laura Ingalls Wilder would never need a Cuisinart. Pioneer and prairie stories convey the fun of roughing it, showing kids how to be self-reliant, or at least less spoiled. 36

Children catch on to the idea of imitating qualities, not literal feats. After returning his storybook to the shelf, little Billy doesn't look around for a dragon to slay. Far-off stories capture the imagination in an abstract but compelling way, different from, say, the more immediate action-adventure flick. After watching a James Bond film festival, I might fantasize about killing the five people in front of me on line at the supermarket, while legends are remote enough that Columbus might inspire one to be original, but not necessarily to study Portuguese or enlist in the navy. In tales about conquerors and cavaliers, I first flirted with the idea of ideas. 37

Even Saturday-morning cartoons served me as parables, when I woke up early enough to watch the classy Superfriends do good deeds. Sure, the gender ratio between Wonder Woman and the gaggle of men in capes seemed unfair, but I was rapt. I wonder whether I glued myself to my television and my high expectations with too much trust, and helped to set my own heroes up for a fall. 38

Some heroes have literally been sentenced to death by their own followers. *Batman* subscribers, for example, were responsible for getting rid of Batman's sidekick, Robin. At the end of one issue, the Joker threatened to kill the Boy Wonder, and readers could decide whether Robin lived or died by calling one of two "900" numbers. The public voted overwhelmingly for his murder. I understand the impulse of those 39 who dialed for death. At a certain point, eternal invincibility grows as dull and predictable as wearing a yellow cape and red tights every day of the year. It's not human. We get fed up.

My generation helped to kill off heroism as teenagers, with our [40] language. We used heroic words that once described brave deeds— *excellent, amazing, awesome* — to describe a good slice of pizza or a sunny day. In our everyday speech, *bad* meant good. *Hot* meant cool. In the sarcastic slang of street gangs in Los Angeles, *hero* currently means traitor, specifically someone who snitches on a graffiti artist.

Even those of us who lived by them helped shatter our own myths, [41] which wasn't all negative. We discovered that even the superhero meets his match. Every Achilles needs a podiatrist. Every rhapsodically handsome leader has a mistress or a moment of moral ambiguity. We injected a dose of reality into our expectations. We even saw a viable presidential candidate under a heap of slung mud, a few imperfections, an alleged tryst or two.

We're used to trysts in a way our elders aren't. Our parents and [42] grandparents behave as if they miss the good old days when adulterers wore letter sweaters. They feign shock at the extramarital exploits of Thomas Jefferson, Frank Sinatra, JFK, Princess Di. Their hero worship is a romance that falters when beloved knights end up unfaithful to their own spouses. People my age aren't amazed by betrayal. We are suspicious of shining armor. Even so, tabloid sales escalate when a Lancelot gives in to temptation—maybe because the jerk who cheats on you somehow becomes more attractive. Other generations have gossiped many of our heroes into philanderers. The presumptuous hero who breaks your heart is the most compelling reason not to get involved in the first place.

Seeing your legends discredited is like ending a romance with [43] someone you loved but ultimately didn't like. However much you longed to trust that person, it just makes more sense not to. Why pine away for an aloof godlet who proves unstable, erratic, and a rotten lover besides? It's sad to give up fantasies but mature to trade them in for healthier relationships grounded in reality.

We require a new pantheon: a set of heroes upon whom we can [44] rely, who will not desert us when the winds change, and whom we will not desert. It's unsettling, if not downright depressing, to go through life embarrassed about the identity of one's childhood idols.

Maybe we should stick to role models instead. Heroes have be- [45] come quaint, as old-fashioned as gas-guzzlers—and as unwieldy, requiring too much investment and energy. Role models are more like compact cars, less glam and roomy but easier to handle. They take up less parking space in the imagination. Role models have a certain degree of consciousness about their job. The cast members of "Beverly Hills 90210," for example, have acknowledged that they serve as role models for adolescents, and their characters behave accordingly: they refrain from committing major crimes; they overcome inclinations toward substance abuse; they see through adult hypocrisy; and any misdemeanors they do perpetrate are punished. For moral mediators we could do better, but at least the prime-time writing staff is aware of the burden of having teen groupies.

Heroes don't have the luxury of staff writers or the opportunity to endorse designer jeans. Hercules can't go on "Nightline" and pledge to stop taking steroids. Prometheus can't get a presidential pardon. Columbus won't have a chance to weep to Barbara Walters that he didn't mean to endanger leatherback turtles or monk seals or the tribes of the Lucayas. Elizabeth I never wrote a best-seller about how she did it her way.

Role models can go on talk shows, or even host them. Role models may live next door. While a hero might be a courageous head of state, a saint, a leader of armies, a role model might be someone who put in a three-day presidential bid, your local minister, your boss. They don't need their planes to go down in flames to earn respect. Role models have a job, accomplishment, or hairstyle worth emulating.

Rather than encompassing the vast kit and caboodle of ideals, role models can perform a little neat division of labor. One could wish to give orders like Norman Schwarzkopf but perform psychoanalysis like Lucy Van Pelt, to chair a round-table meeting as well as King Arthur but negotiate as well as Queen Esther, to eat like Orson Welles but look like Helen of Troy, and so forth. It was General Schwarzkopf, the most tangible military hero for anyone my age, who vied instead for role-model status by claiming on the cover of his book: *It Doesn't Take a Hero.* With this title he modestly implies that anyone with some smarts and élan could strategize and storm as well as he has.

Role models are admirable individuals who haven't given up their lives or livelihoods and may even have a few hang-ups. They don't have to be prone to excessive self-sacrifice. They don't go on hunger strikes; they diet. They are therefore more likely than heroes to be free for lunch, and they are oftener still alive.

Heroism is a living thing for many of my contemporaries. In my informal poll, I not only heard sob stories about the decline of heroes, I also discovered something surprising: the ascent of parents. While the

46

47

48

49

50

founding fathers may be passé, actual mothers, fathers, grands, and great-grands are undeniably "in." An overwhelming number of those I polled named their household forebears as those they most admired. By choosing their own relatives as ideals, people in their twenties have replaced impersonal heroes with the most personal role models of all. Members of my purportedly lost generation have not only realized that it's time to stop believing in Santa Claus, they have chosen to believe instead in their families—the actual tooth fairy, the real Mr. and Mrs. Claus. They have stopped needing the folks from the North Pole, the guys with the wigs, the studs and studettes in tights and capes.

In a way it bodes well that Superman and the rest could be killed or reported missing. They were needed to quash the most villainous folks of all: insane communists bearing nuclear weapons, heinous war criminals, monsters named Doomsday. The good news about Superman bleeding to death was that Doomsday died in the struggle.

If the good guys are gone, so is the world that divides down the middle into good guys and bad guys. A world without heroes is a rigorous, demanding place, where things don't boil down to black and white but are rich with shades of gray; where faith in lofty, dead personages can be replaced by faith in ourselves and one another; where we must summon the strength to imagine a five-dimensional future in colors not yet invented. My generation grew up to see our world shift, so it's up to us to steer a course between naïveté and nihilism, to reshape vintage stories, to create stories of spirit without apologies.

I've heard a few. There was one about the woman who taught Shakespeare to inner-city fourth graders in Chicago who were previously thought to be retarded or hopeless. There was the college groundskeeper and night watchman, a black man with a seventh-grade education, who became a contracts expert, wrote poetry and memoirs, and invested his salary so wisely that he bequeathed 450 acres of mountainous parkland to the university when he died. There was the motorcyclist who slid under an eighteen-wheeler at full speed, survived his physical therapy only to wind up in a plane crash, recovered, and as a disfigured quadriplegic started a business, got happily married, and ran for public office; his campaign button bore a caption that said "Send me to Congress and I won't be just another pretty face. . . ."

When asked for her heroes, a colleague of mine spoke of her great-grandmother, a woman whose husband left her with three kids in Galicia, near Poland, and went to the United States. He meant to send for her, but the First World War broke out. When she made it to America, her husband soon died, and she supported her family; at one point she even ran a nightclub. According to the great-granddaughter, "When she was ninety she would tell me she was going to volunteer at the hospital. I would ask how and she'd say, 'Oh, I just go over there to read to the old folks.' The 'old folks' were probably seventy. She was a great lady."

My grandmother saved her family, too, in the next great war. She 55 did not live to see the age of the fax, but she did see something remarkable in her time, more remarkable even than the emperor riding down the street: she saw him walking down the street. I used to ask her, "Did you really see the emperor Franz Josef walking down the street?"

She would say, "Ya. Walking down the street." I would laugh, and 56 though she'd repeat it to amuse me, she did not see what was so funny. To me, the emperor was someone you met in history books, not on the streets of Vienna. He was larger than life, a surprising pedestrian. He was probably just getting some air, but he was also laying the groundwork for my nostalgia of that time when it would be natural for him to take an evening stroll, when those who were larger than life roamed cobblestones.

Today, life is larger. 57

GOIN' GANGSTA, CHOOSIN' CHOLITA: CLAIMING IDENTITY

Nell Bernstein

■

"GOIN' GANGSTA, CHOOSIN' CHOLITA: CLAIMING IDENTITY" profiles a group of California teenagers who have a very different take on identity, particularly racial and ethnic identity. For them, identity is not a result of nature or nurture; it is a personal choice. This way of thinking about identity has been labeled postmodern, *in contrast to the traditional or modern idea that sees identity as fixed, determined by biology or culture, or by some combination of the two. The postmodern view, on the other hand, treats identity as fluid and flexible. "[I]dentity is not a matter of where you come from, what you were born into, what color your skin is," Bernstein explains. "It's what you wear, the music you listen to, the words you use—everything to which you pledge allegiance, no matter how fleetingly." From a postmodern perspective, identity is performance, a pose you take, a position you occupy.*

For many young people, like the teenagers Bernstein writes about, this postmodern idea of identity is liberating. But for others, postmodernism seems to threaten cherished beliefs and values. As you read this essay, consider why some people are eager to destabilize traditional ideas of identity, while others are troubled by the loss of old certainties.

This essay originally appeared in 1994 in West *magazine, the Sunday supplement to the San Jose* Mercury News. *It was written by San Francisco Bay Area journalist Nell Bernstein. In addition to writing about issues such as AIDS and abortion, Bernstein edits* YO! (Youth Outlook), *a magazine for teenagers published by the Pacific News Service.*

Her lipstick is dark, the lip liner even darker, nearly black.   1
In baggy pants, a blue plaid Pendleton, her bangs pulled back tight off

her forehead, 15-year-old April is a perfect cholita, a Mexican gangsta girl.

But April Miller is Anglo. "And I don't like it!" she complains. "I'd rather be Mexican." 2

April's father wanders into the family room of their home in San Leandro, California, a suburb near Oakland. "Hey, cholita," he teases. "Go get a suntan. We'll put you in a barrio and see how much you like it." 3

A large, sandy-haired man with "April" tattooed on one arm and "Kelly"—the name of his older daughter—on the other, Miller spent 21 years working in a San Leandro glass factory that shut down and moved to Mexico a couple of years ago. He recently got a job in another factory, but he expects NAFTA to swallow that one, too. 4

"Sooner or later we'll all get nailed," he says. "Just another stab in the back of the American middle class." 5

Later, April gets her revenge: "Hey, Mr. White Man's Last Stand," she teases. "Wait till you see how well I manage my welfare check. You'll be asking me for money." 6

A once almost exclusively white, now increasingly Latin and black working-class suburb, San Leandro borders on predominantly black East Oakland. For decades, the boundary was strictly policed and practically impermeable. In 1970 April Miller's hometown was 97 percent white. By 1990 San Leandro was 65 percent white, 6 percent black, 15 percent Hispanic, and 13 percent Asian or Pacific Islander. With minorities moving into suburbs in growing numbers and cities becoming ever more diverse, the boundary between city and suburb is dissolving, and suburban teenagers are changing with the times. 7

In April's bedroom, her past and present selves lie in layers, the pink walls of girlhood almost obscured, Guns N' Roses and Pearl Jam posters overlaid by rappers Paris and Ice Cube. "I don't have a big enough attitude to be a black girl," says April, explaining her current choice of ethnic identification. 8

What matters is that she thinks the choice is hers. For April and her friends, identity is not a matter of where you come from, what you were born into, what color your skin is. It's what you wear, the music you listen to, the words you use—everything to which you pledge allegiance, no matter how fleetingly. 9

The hybridization of American teens has become talk show fodder, with "wiggers"—white kids who dress and talk "black"—appearing on TV in full gangsta regalia. In Indiana a group of white high school girls raised a national stir when they triggered an imitation race 10 war at their virtually all white high school last fall simply by dressing "black."

In many parts of the country, it's television and radio, not neighbors, that introduce teens to the allure of ethnic difference. But in California, which demographers predict will be the first state with no racial majority by the year 2000, the influences are more immediate. The California public schools are the most diverse in the country: 42 percent white, 36 percent Hispanic, 9 percent black, 8 percent Asian. 11

Sometimes young people fight over their differences. Students at virtually any school in the Bay Area can recount the details of at least one "race riot" in which a conflict between individuals escalated into a battle between their clans. More often, though, teens would rather join than fight. Adolescence, after all, is the period when you're most inclined to mimic the power closest at hand, from stealing your older sister's clothes to copying the ruling clique at school. 12

White skaters and Mexican would-be gangbangers listen to gangsta rap and call each other "nigga" as a term of endearment; white girls sometimes affect Spanish accents; blond cheerleaders claim Cherokee ancestors. 13

"Claiming" is the central concept here. A Vietnamese teen in Hayward, another Oakland suburb, "claims" Oakland—and by implication blackness—because he lived there as a child. A law-abiding white kid "claims" a Mexican gang he says he hangs with. A brown-skinned girl with a Mexican father and a white mother "claims" her Mexican side, while her fair-skinned sister "claims" white. The word comes up over and over, as if identity were territory, the self a kind of turf. 14

At a restaurant in a minimall in Hayward, Nicole Huffstutler, 13, sits with her friends and describes herself as "Indian, German, French, Welsh, and, um . . . American": "If somebody says anything like 'Yeah, you're just a peckerwood,' I'll walk up and I'll say 'white pride!' 'Cause I'm proud of my race, and I wouldn't wanna be any other race." 15

"Claiming" white has become a matter of principle for Heather, too, who says she's "sick of the majority looking at us like we're less than them." (Hayward schools were 51 percent white in 1990, down from 77 percent in 1980, and whites are now the minority in many schools.) 16

Asked if she knows that nonwhites have not traditionally been referred to as "the majority" in America, Heather gets exasperated: "I hear that all the time, every day. They say, 'Well, you guys controlled us for many years, and it's time for us to control you.' Every day." 17

When Jennifer Vargas—a small, brown-skinned girl in purple 18 jeans who quietly eats her salad while Heather talks — softly announces that she's "mostly Mexican," she gets in trouble with her friends.

"No, you're not!" scolds Heather. 19

"I'm mostly Indian and Mexican," Jennifer continues flatly. "I'm 20
very little . . . I'm mostly . . ."

"Your mom's white!" Nicole reminds her sharply. "She has blond 21
hair."

"That's what I mean," Nicole adds. "People think that white is a 22
bad thing. They think that white is a bad race. So she's trying to claim more Mexican than white."

"I have very little white in me," Jennifer repeats. "I have mostly 23
my dad's side, 'cause I look like him and stuff. And most of my friends think that me and my brother and sister aren't related, 'cause they look more like my mom."

"But you guys are all the same race, you just look different," 24
Nicole insists. She stops eating and frowns. "OK, you're half and half each what your parents have. So you're equal as your brother and sister, you just look different. And you should be proud of what you are — every little piece and bit of what you are. Even if you were Afghan or whatever, you should be proud of it."

Will Mosley, Heather's 17-year-old brother, says he and his 25
friends listen to rap groups like Compton's Most Wanted, NWA, and Above the Law because they "sing about life" . . . that is, what happens in Oakland, Los Angeles, anyplace but where Will is sitting today, an empty Round Table Pizza in a minimall.

"No matter what race you are," Will says, "if you live like we do, 26
then that's the kind of music you like."

And how do they live? 27

"We don't live bad or anything," Will admits. "We live in a pretty 28
good neighborhood, there's no violence or crime. I was just . . . we're just city people, I guess."

Will and his friend Adolfo Garcia, 16, say they've outgrown try- 29
ing to be something they're not. "When I was 11 or 12," Will says, "I thought I was becoming a big gangsta and stuff. Because I liked that music, and thought it was the coolest, I wanted to become that. I wore big clothes, like you wear in jail. But then I kind of woke up. I looked at myself and thought, 'Who am I trying to be?' "

They may have outgrown blatant mimicry, but Will and his 30
friends remain convinced that they can live in a suburban tract house with a well-kept lawn on a tree-lined street in "not a bad neighborhood"

and still call themselves "city" people on the basis of musical tastes. "City" for these young people means crime, graffiti, drugs. The kids are law-abiding, but these activities connote what Will admiringly calls "action." With pride in his voice, Will predicts that "in a couple of years, Hayward will be like Oakland. It's starting to get more known, because of crime and things. I think it'll be bigger, more things happening, more crime, more graffiti, stealing cars."

"That's good," chimes in 15-year-old Matt Jenkins, whose new 31 beeper—an item that once connoted gangsta chic but now means lit- tle more than an active social life—goes off periodically. "More fun."

The three young men imagine with disdain life in a gangsta-free 32 zone. "Too bland, too boring," Adolfo says. "You have to have some- thing going on. You can't just have everyday life."

"Mowing your lawn," Matt sneers. 33

"Like Beaver Cleaver's house," Adolfo adds. "It's too clean out 34 here."

Not only white kids believe that identity is a matter of choice or 35 taste, or that the power of "claiming" can transcend ethnicity. The Manor Park Locos—a group of mostly Mexican-Americans who hang out in San Leandro's Manor Park—say they descend from the Manor Lords, tough white guys who ruled the neighborhood a generation ago.

They "are like our . . . uncles and dads, the older generation," says 36 Jesse Martinez, 14. "We're what they were when they were around, ex- cept we're Mexican."

"There's three generations," says Oso, Jesse's younger brother. 37 "There's Manor Lords, Manor Park Locos, and Manor Park Pee Wees." The Pee Wees consist mainly of the Locos' younger brothers, eager kids who circle the older boys on bikes and brag about "punking people."

Unlike Will Mosley, the Locos find little glamour in city life. 38 They survey the changing suburban landscape and see not "action" or "more fun" but frightening decline. Though most of them are not yet 18, the Locos are already nostalgic, longing for a Beaver Cleaver past that white kids who mimic them would scoff at.

Walking through nearly empty Manor Park, with its eucalyptus 39 stands, its softball diamond and tennis courts, Jesse's friend Alex, the only Asian in the group, waves his arms in a gesture of futility. "A few years ago, every bench was filled," he says. "Now no one comes here. I guess it's because of everything that's going on. My parents paid a lot for this house, and I want it to be nice for them. I just hope this doesn't turn into Oakland."

Glancing across the park at April Miller's street, Jesse says he 40 knows what the white cholitas are about. "It's not a racial thing," he explains. "It's just all the most popular people out here are Mexican. We're just the gangstas that everyone knows. I guess those girls wanna be known."

Not every young Californian embraces the new racial hybridism. 41 Andrea Jones, 20, an African-American who grew up in the Bay Area suburbs of Union City and Hayward, is unimpressed by what she sees mainly as shallow mimicry. "It's full of posers out here," she says. "When *Boyz N the Hood* came out on video, it was sold out for weeks. The boys all wanna be black, the girls all wanna be Mexican. It's the glamour."

Driving down the quiet, shaded streets of her old neighborhood 42 in Union City, Andrea spots two white preteen boys in Raiders jackets and hugely baggy pants strutting erratically down the empty sidewalk. "Look at them," she says. "Dislocated."

She knows why. "In a lot of these schools out here, it's hard being 43 white," she says. "I don't think these kids were prepared for the backlash that is going on, all the pride now in people of color's ethnicity, and our boldness with it. They have nothing like that, no identity, nothing they can say they're proud of.

"So they latch onto their great-grandmother who's a Cherokee, 44 or they take on the most stereotypical aspects of being black or Mexican. It's beautiful to appreciate different aspects of other people's culture—that's like the dream of what the 21st century should be. But to garnish yourself with pop culture stereotypes just to blend—that's really sad."

Roland Krevocheza, 18, graduated last year from Arroyo High 45 School in San Leandro. He is Mexican on his mother's side, Eastern European on his father's. In the new hierarchies, it may be mixed kids like Roland who have the hardest time finding their place, even as their numbers grow. (One in five marriages in California is between people of different races.) They can always be called "wannabes," no matter what they claim.

"I'll state all my nationalities," Roland says. But he takes a greater 46 interest in his father's side, his Ukrainian, Romanian, and Czech ancestors. "It's more unique," he explains. "Mexican culture is all around me. We eat Mexican food all the time, I hear stories from my grandmother. I see the low-riders and stuff. I'm already part of it. I'm not trying to be; I am."

His darker-skinned brother "says he's not proud to be white," 47 Roland adds. "He calls me 'Mr. Nazi.' " In the room the two share, the American flags and the reproduction of the Bill of Rights are Roland's; the Public Enemy poster belongs to his brother.

Roland has good reason to mistrust gangsta attitudes. In his junior year in high school, he was one of several Arroyo students who were beaten up outside the school at lunchtime by a group of Samoans who came in cars from Oakland. Roland wound up with a split lip, a concussion, and a broken tailbone. Later he was told that the assault was "gang-related"—that the Samoans were beating up anyone wearing red.

"Rappers, I don't like them," Roland says. "I think they're a bad 49 influence on kids. It makes kids think they're all tough and bad."

Those who, like Roland, dismiss the gangsta and cholo styles as 50 affectations can point to the fact that several companies market over-priced knockoffs of "ghetto wear" targeted at teens.

But there's also something going on out here that transcends ado- 51 lescent faddishness and pop culture exoticism. When white kids call their parents "racist" for nagging them about their baggy pants; when they learn Spanish to talk to their boyfriends; when Mexican-American boys feel themselves descended in spirit from white "uncles"; when children of mixed marriages insist that they are whatever race they say they are, all of them are more than just confused.

They're inching toward what Andrea Jones calls "the dream of 52 what the 21st century should be." In the ever more diverse communities of Northern California, they're also facing the complicated reality of what their 21st century will be.

Meanwhile, in the living room of the Miller family's San Lean- 53 dro home, the argument continues unabated. "You don't know what you are," April's father has told her more than once. But she just keeps on telling him he doesn't know what time it is.

WHO AM WE?

Sherry Turkle

.

THIS SELECTION, WHICH ORIGINALLY APPEARED in Wired *magazine (January 1996), comes from Sherry Turkle's latest book,* Life on the Screen: Identity in the Age of the Internet *(1995). Turkle, a professor at MIT's program in science, technology, and society, holds a joint doctorate in psychology and sociology. She likes to describe herself as a "modern woman telling a postmodern tale" about living in cyberspace.*

"Who Am We?" profiles a group of people, like Turkle herself, who engage in role-playing games on the Internet called Multi-User Dungeons (MUDs). MUD players create for themselves virtual identities that are experienced as if they were real. Turkle introduces us to Doug, for example, who plays a "seductive woman" in one game and "a macho, cowboy type" in another. "Cross-dressing" on the Internet allows players not only to masquerade as women or men, but also to become involved in complex relationships with other players who react to them in terms of their virtual gender.

As you read about MUDs and the virtual communities they create, think about what these games can tell us about gender identity in real life (referred to here as RL).

In the early 1970s, the face-to-face role-playing game *Dungeons and Dragons* swept the game culture. The term "dungeon" persisted in the high-tech culture to connote a virtual place. So when virtual spaces were created that many computer users could share and collaborate within, they were deemed Multi-User Dungeons or MUDs, a new kind of social virtual reality. (Some games use software that make them technically MUSHes or MOOs, but the term MUD has come to refer to all of the multi-user environments.)

MUDs are a new kind of virtual parlor game and a new form of community. In addition, text-based MUDs are a new form of collaboratively written literature. MUD players are MUD authors, the creators as well as consumers of media content. In this, participating in a MUD has much in common with scriptwriting, performance art, street theater, improvisational theater, or even commedia del l'arte. But MUDs are something else as well.

As players participate, they become authors not only of text but of themselves, constructing new selves through social interaction. Since one participates in MUDs by sending text to a computer that houses the MUD's program and database, MUD selves are constituted in interaction with the machine. Take it away and the MUD selves cease to exist: "Part of me, a very important part of me, only exists inside PernMUD," says one player. . . .

The anonymity of MUDs gives people the chance to express multiple and often unexplored aspects of the self, to play with their identity and to try out new ones. MUDs make possible the creation of an identity so fluid and multiple that it strains the limits of the notion. Identity, after all, refers to the sameness between two qualities, in this case between a person and his or her persona. But in MUDs, one can be many.

A 21-year-old college senior defends his violent characters as "something in me; but quite frankly I'd rather rape on MUDs where no harm is done." A 26-year-old clerical worker says, "I'm not one thing, I'm many things. Each part gets to be more fully expressed in MUDs than in the real world. So even though I play more than one self on MUDs, I feel more like 'myself' when I'm MUDding." In real life, this woman sees her world as too narrow to allow her to manifest certain aspects of the person she feels herself to be. Creating screen personae is thus an opportunity for self-expression, leading to her feeling more like her true self when decked out in an array of virtual masks.

MUDs imply difference, multiplicity, heterogeneity, and fragmentation. Such an experience of identity contradicts the Latin root of the word, *idem*, meaning "the same." But this contradiction increasingly defines the conditions of our lives beyond the virtual world. MUDs thus become objects-to-think-with for thinking about postmodern selves. Indeed, the unfolding of all MUD action takes place in a resolutely postmodern context. There are parallel narratives in the different rooms of a MUD. The cultures of Tolkien, Gibson, and Madonna coexist and interact. Since MUDs are authored by their players, thousands of people in all, often hundreds at a time, are all logged on from different places; the solitary author is displaced and distributed. Traditional ideas about identity have been tied to a notion of authenticity that such virtual experiences actively subvert. When each player can create many characters in many games, the self is not only decentered but multiplied without limit.

As a new social experience, MUDs pose many psychological questions: If a persona in a role-playing game drops defenses that the player in real life has been unable to abandon, what effect does this have? What if a persona enjoys success in some area (say, flirting) that the player has not been able to achieve? Slippages often occur in places where persona and self merge, where the multiple personae join to comprise what the individual thinks of as his or her authentic self.

7

Doug is a Midwestern college junior. He plays four characters distributed across three different MUDs. One is a seductive woman. One is a macho, cowboy type whose self-description stresses that he is a "Marlboros rolled in the T-shirt sleeve kind of guy." The third is a rabbit of unspecified gender who wanders its MUD introducing people to each other, a character he calls Carrot. Doug says, "Carrot is so low key that people let it be around while they are having private conversations. So I think of Carrot as my passive, voyeuristic character." Doug's fourth character is one that he plays only on a MUD in which all the characters are furry animals. "I'd rather not even talk about that character because my anonymity there is very important to me," Doug says. "Let's just say that on FurryMUDs I feel like a sexual tourist." Doug talks about playing his characters in windows and says that using windows has made it possible for him to "turn pieces of my mind on and off."

8

"I split my mind. . . . I can see myself as being two or three or more. And I just turn on one part of my mind and then another when I go from window to window. I'm in some kind of argument in one window and trying to come on to a girl in a MUD in another, and another window might be running a spreadsheet program or some other technical thing for school. . . . And then I'll get a real-time message that flashes on the screen as soon as it is sent from another system user, and I guess that's RL. RL is just one more window, and it's not usually my best one."

9

Play has always been an important aspect of our individual efforts to build identity. The psychoanalyst Erik Erikson called play a "toy situation" that allows us to "reveal and commit" ourselves "in its unreal-

10

ity." While MUDs are not the only "places" on the Internet in which to play with identity, they provide an unparalleled opportunity for such play. On a MUD one actually gets to build character and environment and then to live within the toy situation. A MUD can become a context for discovering who one is and wishes to be. In this way, the games are laboratories for the construction of identity.

Gender-swapping on MUDs is not a small part of the game action. By some estimates, Habitat, a Japanese MUD, has 1.5 million users. Habitat is a MUD operated for profit. Among the registered members of Habitat, there is a ratio of four real-life men to each real-life woman. But inside the MUD the ratio is only three male characters to one female character. In other words, a significant number of players, many tens of thousands of them, are virtually cross-dressing. 11

What is virtual gender-swapping all about? Some of those who do it claim that it is not particularly significant. "When I play a woman I don't really take it too seriously," said 20-year-old Andrei. "I do it to improve the ratio of women to men. It's just a game." On one level, virtual gender-swapping is easier than doing it in real life. For a man to present himself as female in a chat room, on an IRC channel, or in a MUD, only requires writing a description. For a man to play a woman on the streets of an American city, he would have to shave various parts of his body; wear makeup, perhaps a wig, a dress, and high heels; perhaps change his voice, walk, and mannerisms. He would have some anxiety about passing, and there might be even more anxiety about not passing, which would pose a risk of violence and possibly arrest. So more men are willing to give virtual cross-dressing a try. But once they are online as female, they soon find that maintaining this fiction is difficult. To pass as a woman for any length of time requires understanding how gender inflects speech, manner, the interpretation of experience. Women attempting to pass as men face the same kind of challenge. 12

Virtual cross-dressing is not as simple as Andrei suggests. Not only can it be technically challenging, it can be psychologically complicated. Taking a virtual role may involve you in ongoing relationships. You may discover things about yourself that you never knew before. 13

Case, a 34-year-old industrial designer who is happily married to a co-worker, is currently MUDding as a female character. In response to my question, "Has MUDding ever caused you any emotional pain?" he says, "Yes, but also the kind of learning that comes from hard times. 14

"I'm having pain in my playing now. Mairead, the woman I'm 15

54

playing in MedievalMUSH, is having an interesting relationship with a fellow. Mairead is a lawyer, and the high cost of law school has to be paid for by a corporation or a noble house. She fell in love with a nobleman who paid for her law school. [Case slips into referring to Mairead in the first person.] Now he wants to marry me although I'm a commoner. I finally said yes. I try to talk to him about the fact that I'm essentially his property. I'm a commoner . . . I've grown up with it, that's the way life is. He wants to deny the situation. He says, 'Oh no, no, no. . . . We'll pick you up, set you on your feet, the whole world is open to you.' But every time I behave like I'm now going to be a countess some day . . . as in, 'And I never liked this wallpaper anyway,' I get pushed down. The relationship is pull up, push down. It's an incredibly psychologically damaging thing to do to a person. And the very thing that he liked about her that she was independent, strong, said what was on her mind, it is all being bled out of her."

Case looks at me with a wry smile and sighs, "A woman's life." He continues: "I see her [Mairead] heading for a major psychological problem. What we have is a dysfunctional relationship. But even though it's very painful and stressful, it's very interesting to watch myself cope with this problem. How am I going to dig my persona's self out of this mess? Because I don't want to go on like this. I want to get out of it. . . . You can see that playing this woman lets me see what I have in my psychological repertoire, what is hard and what is easy for me. And I can also see how some of the things that work when you're a man just backfire when you're a woman." [16]

Case further illustrates the complexity of gender swapping as a vehicle for self-reflection. Case describes his RL persona as a nice guy, a "Jimmy Stewart type like my father." He says that in general he likes his father and he likes himself, but he feels he pays a price for his low-key ways. In particular, he feels at a loss when it comes to confrontation, both at home and in business dealings. Case likes MUDding as a female because it makes it easier for him to be aggressive and confrontational. Case plays several online "Katharine Hepburn types," strong, dynamic, "out there" women who remind him of his mother, "who says exactly what's on her mind and is a take-no-prisoners sort." [17]

For Case, if you are assertive as a man, it is coded as "being a bastard." If you are assertive as a woman, it is coded as "modern and together." [18]

Some women who play male characters desire invisibility or permission to be more outspoken or aggressive. "I was born in the South [19]

55

and taught that girls didn't speak up to disagree with men," says Zoe, a 34-year-old woman who plays male and female characters on four MUDs.

"We would sit at dinner and my father would talk and my mother 20
would agree. I thought my father was a god. Once or twice I did disagree with him. I remember one time in particular when I was 10, and he looked at me and said, "Well, well, well, if this little flower grows too many more thorns, she will never catch a man."

Zoe credits MUD with enabling her to reach a state of mind 21
where she is better able to speak up for herself in her marriage ("to say what's on my mind before things get all blown out of proportion") and to handle her job as the financial officer for a small biotechnology firm.

"I played a MUD man for two years. First I did it because I wanted 22
the feeling of an equal playing field in terms of authority, and the only way I could think of to get it was to play a man. But after a while, I got very absorbed by MUDding. I became a wizard on a pretty simple MUD. I called myself Ulysses and got involved in the system and realized that as a man I could be firm and people would think I was a great wizard. As a woman, drawing the line and standing firm has always made me feel like a bitch and, actually, I feel that people saw me as one, too. As a man I was liberated from all that. I learned from my mistakes. I got better at being firm but not rigid. I practiced, safe from criticism."

Zoe's perceptions of her gender trouble are almost the opposite 23
of Case's. While Case sees aggressiveness as acceptable only for women, Zoe sees it as acceptable only for men. These stories share a notion that a virtual gender swap gave people greater emotional range in the real.

The culture of simulation may help us achieve a vision of a mul- 24
tiple but integrated identity whose flexibility, resilience, and capacity for joy comes from having access to our many selves.

THE INTERNET
ENCOURAGES
ISOLATION

Dorothy Chin

■

IN CONTRAST TO SHERRY TURKLE, who shows how role playing games on the Internet can help people learn to empathize with one another and strengthen their sense of a global community, Dorothy Chin suggests that the Internet can have the opposite effect. As a research psychologist at UCLA, Chin sees the Internet as an extension of the gated, ghettoized communities in which many children grow up. She is concerned that as children spend more time at home in front of the computer and less time out in the world actually meeting people from different races and social classes, their belief in stereotypes will grow and their fear of others will increase.

Chin is concerned not only about children but about adults as well. Speaking of her own experience, she observes, "technology only reinforces the barriers in my life that prevent me from meeting and interacting with people." Based on your own experience and observation, what do you think about Chin's concerns?

As I was coasting comfortably along the information super-   1
highway the other day, I was sidetracked by a phone call from a friend. She told me a story involving the 4-year-old daughter of a friend of hers. Awaiting a doctor's appointment, the girl wanted to know if the doctor was "dark" because "dark people" were "scary." The child's mother was appalled; had she somehow communicated this racist stereotype to her daughter? Or had the child picked it up from television?

As I logged off, a thought started to come together. While racist   2
assumptions arguably are deep and institutionalized, there also may be

simpler culprits; limited experience with people outside of one's own ethnic group and faulty reasoning. They go together like this: I've only seen one or two black people (limited experience), and they scared me; if this doctor is black, she also will scare me (faulty reasoning).

Faulty reasoning is normal in children and changes over time as the child's capacity to think develops. Limited experience, however, needs to be combated. If we get to know more people of other ethnic groups, we would be forced to make finer discriminations about them than those based merely on gross physical characteristics such as skin color or eye shape. Racist undertones aside, the idea that "all Asians look alike," for example, is a lumping of people based on the most superficial scanning of their physical features.

3

What is frightening, however, is that chances for getting to know people different from ourselves may be diminishing. How can this be? After all, we are now citizens of the "global village," where our packages can be delivered to the remotest corners of the world in a day, guaranteed, and we're all linked up through long distance lines, faxes and the Internet. But take a look around: People in cities are putting gates around their "communities," ordering takeout and retiring home to their VCRs, using the computer to shop, "chat" with people and take classes. Is it possible that we are getting closer and further apart at the same time? The computer allows me to e-mail friends who otherwise would have been cut adrift, for which I'm thankful, and also to have "conversations" with people I've never met, which makes me uneasy. Whenever I avail myself of this pseudo-social interaction, I suspect it's because I'm too lazy and uncreative to go out and find the real thing. (Web site designers know the real thing is better, too. Why do you think they call their sites "cafes" and typing on the keyboard "chatting"?) The technology only reinforces the barriers in my life that prevent me from meeting and interacting with people — people with whom I can have a real cup of spillable coffee.

4

Of course, the communications technology has opened up the world to some people and connected them in profound ways; for example, the disabled person who is able to communicate much more easily with others. But it can also end up being an instrument of fear. The more we fear venturing outside of our social and geographical comfort zones, the more we rely on technology to get what we need and desire; we can just dial up. And the more technology allows us to do that, the narrower our comfort zones become. None of us knows how this trend ultimately will affect the quality of human relationships, but one potential danger is its impact on race relations in our still-racist society.

5

We already live in segmented neighborhoods that have distinct social boundaries and the new technology can only encourage further isolation. Even if we meet people of different races through the Internet, there is something missing in not being able to see and hear the whole person, with his or her particular skin hue, eye color and shape, speech patterns and mannerisms, all of which enrich and complete the experience.

A few days after my friend's phone call, I read that Bill Gates, the chairman of Microsoft, had endowed a new computer science building on the Stanford campus. Noting the apparent irony of a physical facility in this age of low-cost remote communication, Gates said he felt that technological advances still depended on people getting together face-to-face. I think I will walk over to my friend's house and tell her about it.

6

THE NEW
COMMUNITY

Amitai Etzioni

·

IN THIS SELECTION, SOCIOLOGIST AMITAI ETZIONI gives us a brief history les-
son, explaining how America has evolved from a predominantly rural to an
urban society. He argues that this shift in population from small towns to big
cities, together with increasing economic instability and multicultural tension,
has led to a decline in community feeling.

Etzioni may be nostalgic, but he is not suggesting that we all move back
to the farm. Instead, he wants to inspire us to rebuild a new spirit of commu-
nity for the twenty-first century. The new "Communitarian nexus" Etzioni
envisions consists of many different subcommunities in which people can de-
velop their own identities. But instead of being geographically and culturally
alienated from one another, these subcommunities would work together civilly
to develop shared goals and common bonds.

This selection comes from Etzioni's influential 1993 book, The Spirit
of Community: Rights, Responsibilities, and the Communitarian
Agenda. *As you read the excerpt, you will no doubt notice that Etzioni does*
not detail precisely how to rebuild community along Communitarian lines. As
the book's subtitle indicates, he is more interested in presenting his agenda or
utopian vision than he is in making a practical proposal. As you read the se-
lection, however, you might want to think about what you can do to improve
communication and develop common goals within and between particular sub-
communities in your college, neighborhood, or workplace.

I t's hard to believe now, but for a long time the loss of com-   1
munity was considered to be liberating. Societies were believed to

progress from closely knit, "primitive," or rural villages to unrestrictive, "modern," or urban societies. The former were depicted as based on kinship and loyalty in an age in which both were suspect; the latter, however, were seen as based on reason (or "rationality") in an era in which reason's power to illuminate was admired with little attention paid to the deep shadows it casts. The two types of social relations have often been labeled with the terms supplied by a German sociologist, Ferdinand Tönnies. One is gemeinschaft, the German term for community, and the other is gesellschaft, the German word for society, which he used to refer to people who have rather few bonds, like people in a crowd or a mass society [*Community and Society*].

Far from decrying the loss of community, this sanguine approach   2
to the rise of modernity depicted small towns and villages as backward places that confined behavior. American writers such as Sinclair Lewis and John O'Hara satirized small towns as insular, claustrophobic places, inhabited by petty, mean-spirited people. They were depicted as the opposite of "big cities," whose atmosphere was said to set people free. Anonymity would allow each person to pursue what he or she wished rather than what the community dictated. It was further argued that relations in the gesellschaft would be based not on preexisting, "ascribed" social bonds, such as between cousins, but on contractual relations, freely negotiated among autonomous individuals.

Other major forms of progress were believed to accompany the   3
movement from a world of villages to one of cities. Magic, superstition, alchemy, and religion—"backward beliefs"—would be replaced by bright, shining science and technology. There would be no more villagers willing to sell their wares only to their own kind and not to outsiders—a phenomenon anthropologists have often noted. Old-fashioned values and a sense of obligation were expected to yield to logic and calculation. Social bonds dominating all relations (you did not charge interest on a loan to members of your community because such a charge was considered indecent usury) were pushed aside to make room for a free market, with prices and interest rates set according to market logic. By the same token, the network of reciprocal obligations and care that is at the heart of communities would give way to individual rights protected by the state. The impersonal right to social services and welfare payments, for instance, would replace any reliance on members of one's family, tribe, or ethnic benevolent association.

The sun, moon, and stars of the new universe would be individuals, not the community. In a typical case, the U.S. Supreme Court   4
ruled that the Sierra Club had no legal standing to argue for the preser-

vation of parkland as a community resource (Glendon 112). Rather, if the Sierra Club wished to show standing, it would have to demonstrate that particular individuals were harmed.

Throughout twentieth-century America, as the transition to gesellschaft evolved, even its champions realized that it was not the unmitigated blessing they had expected. Although it was true that those who moved from villages and small towns into urban centers often shed tight social relations and strong community bonds, the result for many was isolation, lack of caring for one another, and exposure to rowdiness and crime.

Criminologists report that young farmhands in rural America in the early nineteenth century did not always work on their parents' land. However, when they were sent to work outside their home they usually lived with other farmers and were integrated into their family life. In this way they were placed in a community context that sustained the moral voice, reinforced the values of their upbringing, and promoted socially constructive behavior. It was only when these farmhands went to work in factories in cities—and were housed on their own in barracks without established social networks, elders, and values—that rowdy and criminal behavior, alcoholism, and prostitution became common. Even in those early days attempts to correct these proclivities were made not by returning these young people to their families and villages, but by trying to generate Communitarian elements in the cities. Among the best analysts of these developments is James Q. Wilson, a leading political scientist. He notes that associations such as the Young Men's Christian Association (YMCA), temperance societies, and the Children's Aid Society sought to provide a socially appropriate, morality-sustaining context for young people ("Rediscovery" 13).

Other experiences paralleled those of the factory hands. The migration to the American West, for example, is usually thought of as a time when individuals were free to venture forth and carve out a life of their own in the Great Plains. Actually, many people traveled in caravans and settled as communities, although each family claimed its own plot of land. Mutual assistance in such rough terrain was an absolute requirement. Mining towns and trading posts, however, in which rampant individualism often did prevail, were places of much chicanery. People who had mined gold often lost their stakes to unscrupulous traders; those who owned land were driven off it with little compensation by railroad companies, among others. Fly-by-night banks frequently welshed on notes that they themselves had issued. An unfettered market, one without a community context, turned out to lack the essential moral underpinnings that trade requires, and not just by sound social relations.

In many ways these frontier settlements — with their washed-out social bonds, loose morals, and unbridled greed — were the forerunners of Wall Street in the 1980s. The Street became a "den of thieves," thick with knaves who held that anything went as long as you made millions more than the next guy. Moreover, the mood of self-centered "making it" of the me generation spilled over into large segments of society. It was celebrated by the White House and many in Congress, who saw in an unfettered pursuit of self-interest the social force that revitalizes economies and societies. By the end of the eighties even some of the proponents of me-ism felt that the pursuit of greed had run amok. 8

By the early nineties the waning of community, which had long concerned sociologists, became more pronounced and drew more attention. As writer Jonathan Rowe put it: "It was common to think about the community as we used to think about air and water. It is there. It takes care of itself, and it can and will absorb whatever we unleash into it" ("Left and Right"). Now it became evident that the social environment needed fostering just as nature did. Responding to the new cues, George Bush evoked the image of a "kinder, gentler" society as a central theme for his first presidential campaign in 1988. The time was right to return to community and the moral order it harbored. Bill Clinton made the spirit of community a theme of his 1992 campaign. 9

The prolonged recession of 1991–1992 and the generally low and slowing growth of the American economy worked against this new concern with we-ness. Interracial and interethnic tensions rose considerably, not only between blacks and whites, but also between blacks and Hispanics and among various segments of the community and Asian-Americans. This is one more reason why the United States will have to work its way to a stronger, growing, more competitive economy: interracial and ethnic peace are much easier to maintain in a rising than in a stagnant economy. However, it does not mean that community rebuilding has to be deferred until the economy is shored up. It does indicate that enhancing we-ness will require greater commitment and effort from both the government and the people, if community rebuilding is to take place in a sluggish economy. 10

Does this mean that we all have to move back to live in small towns and villages in order to ensure the social foundations of morality, to rebuild and shore up we-ness? Can one not bring up decent young people in the city? Isn't it possible to have a modern society, which requires 11 a high concentration of labor and a great deal of geographic mobility—and still sustain a web of social bonds, a Communitarian nexus? There is more than one sociological answer to these queries.

First, many cities have sustained (or reclaimed) some elements of community. Herbert Gans, a Columbia University sociologist, observed that within cities there were what he called "urban villages." He found communities where, generally speaking, "neighbors were friendly and quick to say hello to each other," where the various ethnic groups, transients, and bohemians "could live together side by side without much difficulty." Gans further noted that "for most West Enders [in Boston] . . . life in the area resembled that found in the village or small town, and even in the suburb" (*The Urban Villagers*, 14–15). Even in large metropolises, such as New York City, there are neighborhoods in which many people know their neighbors, their shopkeepers, and their local leaders. They are likely to meet one another in neighborhood bars, bowling alleys, and places of worship. They watch out for each other's safety and children. They act in concert to protect their parks and bus stops. They form political clubs and are a force in local politics. (Jim Sleeper's *Closest of Strangers* provides a fine description of these New York City communities.)

In some instances members of one ethnic group live comfortably next to one another, as in New York City's Chinatown and Miami's Little Havana. In other cities ethnic groups are more geographically dispersed but sustain ethnic-community bonds around such institutions as churches and synagogues, social clubs, and private schools. In recent decades a measure of return to community has benefited from the revival of loyalty to ethnic groups. While the sons and daughters of immigrants, the so-called second generation, often sought to assimilate, to become Americanized to the point that their distinct backgrounds were lost in a new identity, *their* children, the third generation and onward, often seek to reestablish their ethnic identity and bonds.

How does one reconcile the two sociological pictures—the James Q. Wilson concept of the city as gesellschaft, with little community or moral base, and the Herbert Gans image of gemeinschaft, of urban villages? The answer, first of all, is that both exist side by side. Between the urban villages, in row houses and high rises, you find large pockets of people who do not know their next-door neighbors, with whom they may have shared a floor, corridors, and elevators for a generation. Elderly people especially, who have no social bonds at work and are largely abandoned by their families, often lead rather isolated lives. In 1950 14.4 percent of those sixty-five years of age and older lived alone (Monk 534);

by 1990 the percentage stood at nearly 31 percent (U.S. Bureau of the Census, Table L, 12).

Also, to some extent a welcome return to small-town life of sorts 15 has been occurring in modern America. Although not all suburbs, which attracted millions of city dwellers, make for viable communities, as a rule the movement to the suburbs has enhanced the Communitarian nexus.

In addition, postmodern technology helps. More people are again 16 able to work at home or nearby, and a high concentration of labor is less and less necessary, in contrast with the industrial age. People can use their computers and modems at home to do a good part of their office work, from processing insurance claims to trading worldwide in commodities, stocks, and bonds. Architects can design buildings and engineers monitor faraway power networks from their places of residence.

It used to be widely observed that Americans, unlike Europeans, 17 move around so much that they are hard-pressed to put down real community roots. On average, it is said, the whole country moves about once every five years. These figures, however, may be a bit obsolete. For various reasons, in recent years Americans seem to move somewhat less often (Barringer A16). One explanation is a growing desire to maintain the bonds of friendship and local social roots of their children, spouses, and themselves. In effect there is little reason to believe that the economy will suffer if this trend continues, and it may actually benefit from less shuttling around of people. Surely the Communitarian nexus will benefit.

Finally, there are new, nongeographic, communities made up of 18 people who do not live near one another. Their foundations may not be as stable and deep-rooted as residential communities, but they fulfill many of the social and moral functions of traditional communities. Work-based and professional communities are among the most common of these. That is, people who work together in a steel mill or a high-tech firm such as Lotus or Microsoft often develop work-related friendships and community webs; groups of co-workers hang around together, help one another, play and party together, and go on joint outings. As they learn to know and care for one another, they also form and reinforce moral expectations.

Other communities are found in some law firms, on many cam- 19 puses (although one community may not encompass everyone on campus), among physicians at the same hospital or with the same specialty in a town, and among some labor union members.

Some critics have attacked these communities as being artificially 20 constructed, because they lack geographical definition or because they are merely social networks, without a residential concentration. Ray Oldenburg, author of *The Great Good Place*, decries the new definitions of community that encompass co-workers and even radio call-in show audiences. "Can we really create a satisfactory community apart from geography?" he asks (Baldwin 17). "My answer is 'no.' " But people who work every day in the same place spend more hours together and in closer proximity than people who live on the same village street. Most important, these nongeographic communities often provide at least some elements of the Communitarian nexus, and hence they tend to have the moral infrastructure we consider essential for a civil and humane society.

In short, our society is neither without community nor sufficiently Communitarian; it is neither gemeinschaft nor gesellschaft, but a mixture of the two sociological conditions. America does not need a simple return to gemeinschaft, to the traditional community. Modern economic prerequisites preclude such a shift, but even if it were possible, such backpedaling would be undesirable because traditional communities have been too constraining and authoritarian. Such traditional communities were usually homogeneous. What we need now are communities that balance both diversity and unity. As John W. Gardner has noted: "To prevent the wholeness from smothering diversity, there must be a philosophy of pluralism, an open climate for dissent, and an opportunity for subcommunities to retain their identity and share in the setting of larger group goals" (*Building Community* 11). Thus, we need to strengthen the communitarian elements in the urban and suburban centers, to provide the social bonds that sustain the moral voice, but at the same time avoid tight networks that suppress pluralism and dissent. James Pinkerton, who served in the Bush White House, speaks eloquently about a new paradigm focused around what he calls a "new gemeinschaft." It would be, he says, neither oppressive nor hierarchical. In short, we need new communities in which people have choices and readily accommodate divergent *sub*communities but still maintain common bonds.

21

Notes

Deborah Baldwin, "Creating Community," *Common Cause Magazine*, July/August 1990, 17.

Felicity Barringer, "18 percent of Households in U.S. Moved in '89," *New York Times*, December 20, 1991, A16.

Herbert Gans, *The Urban Villagers: Group and Class in the Life of Italian-Americans* (New York: The Free Press, 1962, 1982), 14–15.

John W. Gardner, *Building Community* (Washington, D.C.: Independent Sector, 1991), 11.

Mary Ann Glendon, *Rights Talk* (New York: The Free Press, 1991), 112.

Abraham Monk, "Aging, Loneliness, and Communications," *American Behavioral Scientist* 31(5): 534.

Jonathan Rowe, "Left and Right: The Emergence of a New Politics in the 1990s?" sponsored by the Heritage Foundation and the Progressive Foundation, October 30, 1991, Washington, D.C.

Jim Sleeper, *Closest of Strangers: Liberalism and the Politics of Race in New York* (New York: W. W. Norton & Company, 1990).

Ferdinand Tönnies, *Community and Society*, translated and edited by Charles P. Loomis (East Lansing: Michigan State University Press, 1957).

U.S. Bureau of the Census, Current Population Reports, series P–20, no. 450, *Marital Status and Living Arrangements: March 1990* (Washington, D.C.: U.S. Government Printing Office, 1991), table L, 12.

James Q. Wilson, "The Rediscovery of Character: Private Virtue and Public Policy," *The Public Interest* 81 (Fall 1985): 13.

THE LOTTERY

Shirley Jackson

∎

SHIRLEY JACKSON (1919–1965) WROTE many stories and novels but is best known for "The Lottery," which has been widely anthologized as well as performed in television, theater, and film. From its initial appearance in The New Yorker *magazine on June 28, 1948, "The Lottery" has generated a lot of controversy.* More people wrote to The New Yorker *to comment on Jackson's story than had ever written the magazine before and, as Jackson has pointed out, few people liked it—including her agent, editor, and parents, who criticized her for writing a "gloomy" story instead of one that would "cheer people up."*

Before reading "The Lottery," you might recall the opening paragraphs of Amitai Etzioni's essay "The New Community" in which he alludes to the nostalgia felt by many people today for the comfortable intimacy and security of traditional small town life. As you read "The Lottery," note how Jackson fosters this nostalgic view. But note also how her story embodies what Etzioni describes as the modern view of "small towns and villages as backward places that confined behavior," places where "backward beliefs" like "magic, superstition, alchemy, and religion" prevailed. Jackson has explained that she had "hoped, by setting a particularly brutal ancient rite in the present and in [her] own village, to shock the story's readers." What effect does the story have as you read it a half-century later? What does it make you think about small communities where everyone knows your name?*

---

*Quoted by Ann Charters in *The Story and Its Writer* (St. Martin's Press, 1983, p. 942).

Τhe morning of June 27th was clear and sunny, with the fresh   1
warmth of a full-summer day; the flowers were blossoming profusely
and the grass was richly green. The people of the village began to
gather in the square, between the post office and the bank, around ten
o'clock; in some towns there were so many people that the lottery took
two days and had to be started on June 26th, but in this village, where
there were only about three hundred people, the whole lottery took less
than two hours, so it could begin at ten o'clock in the morning and still
be through in time to allow the villagers to get home for noon dinner.

The children assembled first, of course. School was recently over   2
for the summer, and the feeling of liberty sat uneasily on most of them;
they tended to gather together quietly for a while before they broke into
boisterous play, and their talk was still of the classroom and the teacher,
of books and reprimands. Bobby Martin had already stuffed his pockets full of stones, and the other boys soon followed his example, se-
lecting the smoothest and roundest stones; Bobby and Harry Jones and
Dickie Delacroix—the villagers pronounced this name "Dellacroy"—
eventually made a great pile of stones in one corner of the square and
guarded it against the raids of the other boys. The girls stood aside, talking among themselves, looking over their shoulders at the boys, and the
very small children rolled in the dust or clung to the hands of their older
brothers or sisters.

Soon the men began to gather, surveying their own children,   3
speaking of planting and rain, tractors and taxes. They stood together,
away from the pile of stones in the corner, and their jokes were quiet
and they smiled rather than laughed. The women, wearing faded house
dresses and sweaters, came shortly after their menfolk. They greeted
one another and exchanged bits of gossip as they went to join their husbands. Soon the women, standing by their husbands, began to call to
their children, and the children came reluctantly, having to be called
four or five times. Bobby Martin ducked under his mother's grasping
hand and ran, laughing, back to the pile of stones. His father spoke up
sharply, and Bobby came quickly and took his place between his father
and his oldest brother.

The lottery was conducted—as were the square dances, the teen-   4
age club, the Halloween program—by Mr. Summers, who had time and
energy to devote to civic activities. He was a round-faced, jovial man
and he ran the coal business, and people were sorry for him, because
he had no children and his wife was a scold. When he arrived in the

square, carrying the black wooden box, there was a murmur of conversation among the villagers, and he waved and called, "Little late today, folks." The postmaster, Mr. Graves, followed him, carrying a three-legged stool, and the stool was put in the center of the square and Mr. Summers set the black box down on it. The villagers kept their distance, leaving a space between themselves and the stool, and when Mr. Summers said, "Some of you fellows want to give me a hand?" there was a hesitation before two men, Mr. Martin and his oldest son, Baxter, came forward to hold the box steady on the stool while Mr. Summers stirred up the papers inside it.

The original paraphernalia for the lottery had been lost long ago, and the black box now resting on the stool had been put into use even before Old Man Warner, the oldest man in town, was born. Mr. Summers spoke frequently to the villagers about making a new box, but no one liked to upset even as much tradition as was represented by the black box. There was a story that the present box had been made with some pieces of the box that had preceded it, the one that had been constructed when the first people settled down to make a village here. Every year, after the lottery, Mr. Summers began talking again about a new box, but every year the subject was allowed to fade off without anything's being done. The black box grew shabbier each year; by now it was no longer completely black but splintered badly along one side to show the original wood color, and in some places faded or stained.

Mr. Martin and his oldest son, Baxter, held the black box securely on the stool until Mr. Summers had stirred the papers thoroughly with his hand. Because so much of the ritual had been forgotten or discarded, Mr. Summers had been successful in having slips of paper substituted for the chips of wood that had been used for generations. Chips of wood, Mr. Summers had argued, had been all very well when the village was tiny, but now that the population was more than three hundred and likely to keep on growing, it was necessary to use something that would fit more easily into the black box. The night before the lottery, Mr. Summers and Mr. Graves made up the slips of paper and put them in the box, and it was then taken to the safe of Mr. Summers' coal company and locked up until Mr. Summers was ready to take it to the square next morning. The rest of the year, the box was put away, sometimes one place, sometimes another; it had spent one year in Mr. Graves's barn and another year underfoot in the post office, and sometimes it was set on a shelf in the Martin grocery and left there.

There was a great deal of fussing to be done before Mr. Summers declared the lottery open. There were the lists to make up—of heads of families, heads of households in each family, members of each household in each family. There was the proper swearing-in of Mr. Summers by the postmaster, as the official of the lottery; at one time, some people remembered, there had been a recital of some sort, performed by the official of the lottery, a perfunctory, tuneless chant that had been rattled off duly each year; some people believed that the official of the lottery used to stand just so when he said or sang it, others believed that he was supposed to walk among the people, but years and years ago this part of the ritual had been allowed to lapse. There had been, also, a ritual salute, which the official of the lottery had had to use in addressing each person who came up to draw from the box, but this also had changed with time, until now it was felt necessary only for the official to speak to each person approaching. Mr. Summers was very good at all this; in his clean white shirt and blue jeans, with one hand resting carelessly on the black box, he seemed very proper and important as he talked interminably to Mr. Graves and the Martins.

Just as Mr. Summers finally left off talking and turned to the assembled villagers, Mrs. Hutchinson came hurriedly along the path to the square, her sweater thrown over her shoulders, and slid into place in the back of the crowd. "Clean forgot what day it was," she said to Mrs. Delacroix, who stood next to her, and they both laughed softly. "Thought my old man was out back stacking wood," Mrs. Hutchinson went on, "and then I looked out the window and the kids were gone, and then I remembered it was the twenty-seventh and came a-running." She dried her hands on her apron, and Mrs. Delacroix said, "You're in time, though. They're still talking away up there."

Mrs. Hutchinson craned her neck to see through the crowd and found her husband and children standing near the front. She tapped Mrs. Delacroix on the arm as a farewell and began to make her way through the crowd. The people separated good-humoredly to let her through; two or three people said, in voices just loud enough to be heard across the crowd, "Here comes your Missus, Hutchinson," and "Bill, she made it after all." Mrs. Hutchinson reached her husband, and Mr. Summers, who had been waiting, said cheerfully, "Thought we were going to have to get on without you, Tessie." Mrs. Hutchinson said, grinning, "Wouldn't have me leave m'dishes in the sink, now, would you, Joe?" and soft laughter ran through the crowd as the people stirred back into position after Mrs. Hutchinson's arrival.

"Well, now," Mr. Summers said soberly, "guess we better get started, get this over with, so's we can go back to work. Anybody ain't here?"

8

9

10

71

"Dunbar," several people said. "Dunbar, Dunbar." 11

Mr. Summers consulted his list. "Clyde Dunbar," he said. "That's 12 right. He's broke his leg, hasn't he? Who's drawing for him?"

"Me, I guess," a woman said, and Mr. Summers turned to look at 13 her. "Wife draws for her husband," Mr. Summers said. "Don't you have a grown boy to do it for you, Janey?" Although Mr. Summers and everyone else in the village knew the answer perfectly well, it was the business of the official of the lottery to ask such questions formally. Mr. Summers waited with an expression of polite interest while Mrs. Dunbar answered.

"Horace's not but sixteen yet," Mrs. Dunbar said regretfully. 14 "Guess I gotta fill in for the old man this year."

"Right," Mr. Summers said. He made a note on the list he was 15 holding. Then he asked, "Watson boy drawing this year?"

A tall boy in the crowd raised his hand. "Here," he said. "I'm draw- 16 ing for m'mother and me." He blinked his eyes nervously and ducked his head as several voices in the crowd said things like "Good fellow, Jack," and "Glad to see your mother's got a man to do it."

"Well," Mr. Summers said, "guess that's everyone. Old Man 17 Warner make it?"

"Here," a voice said, and Mr. Summers nodded. 18

A sudden hush fell on the crowd as Mr. Summers cleared his 19 throat and looked at the list. "All ready?" he called. "Now, I'll read the names—heads of families first—and the men come up and take a paper out of the box. Keep the paper folded in your hand without looking at it until everyone has had a turn. Everything clear?"

The people had done it so many times that they only half listened 20 to the directions; most of them were quiet, wetting their lips, not looking around. Then Mr. Summers raised one hand high and said, "Adams." A man disengaged himself from the crowd and came forward. "Hi, Steve," Mr. Summers said, and Mr. Adams said, "Hi, Joe." They grinned at one another humorlessly and nervously. Then Mr. Adams reached into the black box and took out a folded paper. He held it firmly by one corner as he turned and went hastily back to his place in the crowd, where he stood a little apart from his family, not looking down at his hand.

"Allen," Mr. Summers said. "Anderson . . . Bentham." 21

"Seems like there's no time at all between lotteries any more," 22 Mrs. Delacroix said to Mrs. Graves in the back row. "Seems like we got through with the last one only last week."

"Time sure goes fast," Mrs. Graves said. 23

"Clark . . . Delacroix." 24

"There goes my old man," Mrs. Delacroix said. She held her 25
breath while her husband went forward.

"Dunbar," Mr. Summers said, and Mrs. Dunbar went steadily to 26
the box while one of the women said, "Go on, Janey," and another said,
"There she goes."

"We're next," Mrs. Graves said. She watched while Mr. Graves 27
came around from the side of the box, greeted Mr. Summers gravely,
and selected a slip of paper from the box. By now, all through the crowd
there were men holding the small folded papers in their large hands,
turning them over and over nervously. Mrs. Dunbar and her two sons
stood together, Mrs. Dunbar holding the slip of paper.

"Harburt . . . Hutchinson." 28

"Get up there, Bill," Mrs. Hutchinson said, and the people near 29
her laughed.

"Jones." 30

"They do say," Mr. Adams said to Old Man Warner, who stood 31
next to him, "that over in the north village they're talking of giving up
the lottery."

Old Man Warner snorted. "Pack of crazy fools," he said. "Lis- 32
tening to the young folks, nothing's good enough for *them*. Next thing
you know, they'll be wanting to go back to living in caves, nobody work
any more, live *that* way for a while. Used to be a saying about 'Lottery
in June, corn be heavy soon.' First thing you know, we'd all be eating
stewed chickweed and acorns. There's *always* been a lottery," he added
petulantly. "Bad enough to see young Joe Summers up there joking with
everybody."

"Some places have already quit lotteries," Mrs. Adams said. 33

"Nothing but trouble in *that*," Old Man Warner said stoutly. 34
"Pack of young fools."

"Martin." And Bobby Martin watched his father go forward. 35
"Overdyke . . . Percy."

"I wish they'd hurry," Mrs. Dunbar said to her older son. "I wish 36
they'd hurry."

"They're almost through," her son said. 37

"You get ready to run tell Dad," Mrs. Dunbar said. 38

Mr. Summers called his own name and then stepped forward pre- 39
cisely and selected a slip from the box. Then he called, "Warner."

"Seventy-seventh year I been in the lottery," Old Man Warner 40
said as he went through the crowd. "Seventy-seventh time."

"Watson." The tall boy came awkwardly through the crowd. 41

Someone said, "Don't be nervous, Jack," and Mr. Summers said, "Take your time, son."

"Zanini." 42

After that, there was a long pause, a breathless pause, until Mr. 43
Summers, holding his slip of paper in the air, said, "All right, fellows."
For a minute, no one moved, and then all the slips of paper were
opened. Suddenly, all the women began to speak at once, saying, "Who
is it?" "Who's got it?" "Is it the Dunbars?" "Is it the Watsons?" Then
the voices began to say, "It's Hutchinson. It's Bill," "Bill Hutchinson's
got it."

"Go tell your father," Mrs. Dunbar said to her older son. 44

People began to look around to see the Hutchinsons. Bill 45
Hutchinson was standing quiet, staring down at the paper in his hand.
Suddenly, Tessie Hutchinson shouted to Mr. Summers, "You didn't
give him time enough to take any paper he wanted. I saw you. It wasn't
fair."

"Be a good sport, Tessie." Mrs. Delacroix called, and Mrs. Graves 46
said, "All of us took the same chance."

"Shut up, Tessie," Bill Hutchinson said. 47

"Well, everyone," Mr. Summers said, "that was done pretty fast, 48
and now we've got to be hurrying a little more to get done in time." He
consulted his next list. "Bill," he said, "you draw for the Hutchinson
family. You got any other households in the Hutchinsons?"

"There's Don and Eva," Mrs. Hutchinson yelled. "Make *them* take 49
their chance!"

"Daughters draw with their husband's families, Tessie," Mr. Sum- 50
mers said gently. "You know that as well as anyone else."

"It wasn't *fair*," Tessie said. 51

"I guess not, Joe," Bill Hutchinson said regretfully. "My daugh- 52
ter draws with her husband's family, that's only fair. And I've got no
other family except the kids."

"Then, as far as drawing for families is concerned, it's you," Mr. 53
Summers said in explanation, "and as far as drawing for households is
concerned, that's you, too. Right?"

"Right," Bill Hutchinson said. 54

"How many kids, Bill?" Mr. Summers asked formally. 55

"Three," Bill Hutchinson said. "There's Bill, Jr., and Nancy, and 56
little Dave. And Tessie and me."

"All right, then," Mr. Summers said. "Harry, you got their tick- 57
ets back?"

Mr. Graves nodded and held up the slips of paper. "Put them in   58
the box, then," Mr. Summers directed. "Take Bill's and put it in."

"I think we ought to start over," Mrs. Hutchinson said, as quietly   59
as she could. "I tell you it wasn't *fair*. You didn't give him time enough
to choose. *Every*body saw that."

Mr. Graves had selected the five slips and put them in the box,   60
and he dropped all the papers but those onto the ground, where the
breeze caught them and lifted them off.

"Listen, everybody," Mrs. Hutchinson was saying to the people   61
around her.

"Ready, Bill?" Mr. Summers asked, and Bill Hutchinson, with one   62
quick glance around at his wife and children, nodded.

"Remember," Mr. Summers said, "take the slips and keep them   63
folded until each person has taken one. Harry, you help little Dave."
Mr. Graves took the hand of the little boy, who came willingly with him
up to the box. "Take a paper out of the box, Davy," Mr. Summers said.
Davy put his hand into the box and laughed. "Take just *one* paper," Mr.
Summers said. "Harry, you hold it for him." Mr. Graves took the child's
hand and removed the folded paper from the tight fist and held it while
little Dave stood next to him and looked up at him wonderingly.

"Nancy next," Mr. Summers said. Nancy was twelve, and her   64
school friends breathed heavily as she went forward, switching her skirt,
and took a slip daintily from the box. "Bill, Jr.," Mr. Summers said, and
Billy, his face red and his feet over-large, nearly knocked the box over
as he got a paper out. "Tessie," Mr. Summers said. She hesitated for a
minute, looking around defiantly, and then set her lips and went up to
the box. She snatched a paper out and held it behind her.

"Bill," Mr. Summers said, and Bill Hutchinson reached into the   65
box and felt around, bringing his hand out at last with the slip of paper
in it.

The crowd was quiet. A girl whispered, "I hope it's not Nancy,"   66
and the sound of the whisper reached the edges of the crowd.

"It's not the way it used to be," Old Man Warner said clearly.   67
"People ain't the way they used to be."

"All right," Mr. Summers said. "Open the papers. Harry, you   68
open little Dave's."

Mr. Graves opened the slip of paper and there was a general sigh   69
through the crowd as he held it up and everyone could see that it was
blank. Nancy and Bill, Jr., opened theirs at the same time, and both
beamed and laughed, turning around to the crowd and holding their
slips of paper above their heads.

"Tessie," Mr. Summers said. There was a pause, and then Mr. 70
Summers looked at Bill Hutchinson, and Bill unfolded his paper and
showed it. It was blank.

"It's Tessie," Mr. Summers said, and his voice was hushed. "Show 71
us her paper, Bill."

Bill Hutchinson went over to his wife and forced the slip of paper 72
out of her hand. It had a black spot on it, the black spot Mr. Summers
had made the night before with the heavy pencil in the coal-company
office. Bill Hutchinson held it up, and there was a stir in the crowd.

"All right, folks," Mr. Summers said. "Let's finish quickly." 73

Although the villagers had forgotten the ritual and lost the orig- 74
inal black box, they still remembered to use stones. The pile of stones
the boys had made earlier was ready; there were stones on the ground
with the blowing scraps of paper that had come out of the box. Mrs.
Delacroix selected a stone so large she had to pick it up with both hands
and turned to Mrs. Dunbar. "Come on," she said. "Hurry up."

Mrs. Dunbar had small stones in both hands, and she said, gasp- 75
ing for breath, "I can't run at all. You'll have to go ahead and I'll catch
up with you."

The children had stones already, and someone gave little Davy 76
Hutchinson a few pebbles.

Tessie Hutchinson was in the center of a cleared space by now, 77
and she held her hands out desperately as the villagers moved in on her.
"It isn't fair," she said. A stone hit her on the side of the head.

Old Man Warner was saying, "Come on, come on, everyone." 78
Steve Adams was in the front of the crowd of villagers, with Mrs. Graves
beside him.

"It isn't fair, it isn't right," Mrs. Hutchinson screamed, and then 79
they were upon her.

AMERICA'S EMERGING GAY CULTURE

Randall E. Majors

■

THIS ESSAY EXAMINES THE PATTERNS *of communication that form one particular subcommunity, contemporary American gay culture. Written for an academic audience, it originally appeared in* Intercultural Communication *(1991), a linguistics anthology. Randall E. Majors, a professor at California State University at Hayward, has also written an introductory textbook,* Basic Speech Communication *(1987).*

Majors looks at four elements of communication in the gay community. Beginning at the neighborhood level, he discusses the way a particular locale becomes known as gay and how that designation reinforces individual identity as well as group cohesion. Then he focuses on specialized groups to show how they satisfy the need for affiliation while at the same time provide a safe haven. Turning to the role of language, Majors explains how symbols are used within the gay community as well as within the larger heterosexual community. The final aspect of communication he analyzes is the essentially nonverbal meeting behavior called "cruising."

You might be interested in doing an analysis of your own based on Majors's essay. Consider, for example, analyzing some aspect of communication within your family or among a group of friends or coworkers. You might look at verbal or nonverbal ways in which the group members establish or reinforce their allegiance to or their power over one another.

Agay culture, unique in the history of homosexuality, is   1
emerging in America. Gay people from all walks of life are forging new
self-identity concepts, discovering new political and social power, and

building a revolutionary new life style. As more people "come out," identify themselves as gay, and join with others to work and live as openly gay people, a stronger culture takes shape with each passing year.

There have always been homosexual men and women, but never before has there emerged the notion of a distinct "culture" based on being gay. A useful way to analyze this emerging gay culture is to observe the communication elements by which gay people construct their life styles and social institutions. Lesbians and gay men, hereafter considered together as gay people, are creating a new community in the midst of the American melting pot. They are building social organizations, exercising political power, and solidifying a unique sense of identity—often under repressive and sometimes dangerous conditions. The following essay is an analysis of four major communication elements of the American gay culture: the gay neighborhood, gay social groups, gay symbols, and gay meeting behavior. These communication behaviors will demonstrate the vibrancy and joy that a new culture offers the American vision of individual freedom and opportunity.

THE GAY NEIGHBORHOOD

Most cultural groups find the need to mark out a home turf. American social history has many examples of ethnic and social groups who create their own special communities, whether by withdrawing from the larger culture or by forming specialized groups within it. The utopian communities of the Amish or Shakers are examples of the first, and ghetto neighborhoods in large urban areas are examples of the latter.

This need to create a group territory fulfills several purposes for gay people. First, a gay person's sense of identity is reinforced if there is a special place that is somehow imbued with "gayness." When a neighborhood becomes the home of many gay people, the ground is created for a feeling of belonging and sharing with others. Signs of gayness, whether overt symbols like rainbow flags or more subtle cues such as merely the presence of other gay people on the street, create the feeling that a certain territory is special to the group and hospitable to the group's unique values.

How do you know when a neighborhood is gay? As with any generality, the rule of thumb is that "enough gay people in a neighborhood and it becomes a gay neighborhood." Rarely do gay people want to paint the streetlamps lavender, but the presence of many more subtle factors gives a gay character to an area. The most subtle cues are the presence of gay people as they take up residence in a district. Word spreads in the group that a certain area is starting to look attractive and open to gay members. There is often a move to "gentrify" older, more affordable sections of a city and build a new neighborhood out of the leftovers from the rush to the suburbs. Gay businesses, those operated by or catering to gay people, often develop once enough clientele is in the area. Social groups and services emerge that are oriented toward the members of the neighborhood. Eventually, the label of "gay neighborhood" is placed on an area, and the transformation is complete. The Castro area in San Francisco, Greenwich Village in New York, New Town in Chicago, the Westheimer district in Houston, and West Hollywood or Silver Lake in Los Angeles are examples of the many emergent gay neighborhoods in cities across America.

A second need fulfilled by the gay neighborhood is the creation   6
of a meeting ground. People can recognize and meet each other more easily when a higher density of like population is established. It is not easy to grow up gay in America; gay people often feel "different" because of their sexual orientations. The surrounding heterosexual culture often tries to imprint on everyone sexual behaviors and expectations that do not suit gay natures. Because of this pressure, gay people often feel isolated and alienated, and the need for a meeting ground is very important. Merely knowing that there is a specific place where other gay people live and work and play does much to anchor the psychological aspect of gayness in a tangible, physical reality. A gay person's sense of identity is reinforced by knowing that there is a home base, or a safe place where others of a similar persuasion are nearby.

Gay neighborhoods reinforce individual identity by focusing activities and events for members of the group. Celebrations of group   7
unity and pride, demonstrations of group creativity and accomplishment, and services to individual members' needs are more easily developed when they are centralized. Gay neighborhoods are host to all the outward elements of a community — parades, demonstrations, car washes, basketball games, petition signing, street fairs, and garage sales.

A critical purpose for gay neighborhoods is that of physical and   8
psychological safety. Subcultural groups usually experience some degree of persecution and oppression from the larger surrounding culture. For gay people, physical safety is a very real concern — incidences of homophobic assaults or harassment are common in most American cities. By centralizing gay activities, some safeguards can be mounted, as large numbers of gay people living in proximity create a deterrence to violence. This may be informal awareness of the need to take extra

precautions and to be on the alert to help other gay people in distress or in the form of actual street patrols or social groups, such as Community United Against Violence in San Francisco. A sense of psychological safety follows from these physical measures. Group consciousness raising on neighborhood safety and training in safety practices create a sense of group cohesion. The security inspired by the group thus creates a psychic comfort that offsets the paranoia that can be engendered by alienation and individual isolation.

Another significant result of gay neighborhoods is the political reality of "clout." In the context of American grassroots democracy, a predominantly gay population in an area can lead to political power. The concerns of gay people are taken more seriously by politicians and elected officials representing an area where voters can be registered and mustered into service during elections. In many areas, openly gay politicians represent gay constituencies directly and voice their concerns in ever-widening forums. The impact of this kind of democracy-in-action is felt on other institutions as well: police departments, social welfare agencies, schools, churches, and businesses. When a group centralizes its energy, members can bring pressure to bear on other cultural institutions, asking for and demanding attention to the unique needs of that group. Since American culture has a strong tradition of cultural diversity, gay neighborhoods are effective agents in the larger cultural acceptance of gay people. The gay rights movement, which attempts to secure housing, employment, and legal protection for gay people, finds its greatest support in the sense of community created by gay neighborhoods.

GAY SOCIAL GROUPS

On a smaller level than the neighborhood, specialized groups fulfill the social needs of gay people. The need for affiliation—to make friends, to share recreation, to find life partners, or merely to while away the time—is a strong drive in any group of people. Many gay people suffer from an isolation caused by rejection by other people or by their own fear of being discovered as belonging to an unpopular group. This homophobia leads to difficulty in identifying and meeting other gay people who can help create a sense of dignity and caring. This is particularly true for gay teenagers who have limited opportunities to meet other gay people. Gay social groups serve the important function of helping gay people locate each other so that this affiliation need can be met.

The development of gay social groups depends to a large degree 11
on the number of gay people in an area and the perceived risk factor.
In smaller towns and cities, there are often no meeting places, which
exacerbates the problem of isolation. In some small towns a single business may be the only publicly known meeting place for gay people
within hundreds of miles. In larger cities, however, an elaborate array
of bars, clubs, social groups, churches, service agencies, entertainment
groups, stores, restaurants, and the like add to the substance of a gay
culture.

The gay bar is often the first public gay experience for a gay per- 12
son, and it serves as a central focus for many people. Beyond the personal need of meeting potential relationship partners, the gay bar also
serves the functions of entertainment and social activity. Bars offer a
wide range of attractions suited to gay people: movies, holiday celebrations, dancing, costume parties, live entertainment, free meals, boutiques, and meeting places for social groups. Uniquely gay forms of entertainment, such as drag shows and disco dancing, were common in
gay bars before spreading into the general culture. Bars often become
a very central part of a community's social life by sponsoring athletic
teams, charities, community services, and other events as well as serving as meeting places.

The centrality of the bar in gay culture has several drawbacks, 13
however. Young gay people are denied entrance because of age re-
strictions, and there may be few other social outlets for them. A high
rate of alcoholism among urban gay males is prominent. With the
spread of Acquired Immune Deficiency Syndrome (AIDS), the use of
bars for meeting sexual partners has declined dramatically as gay people turn to developing more permanent relationships.

Affiliation needs remain strong despite these dangers, however, 14
and alternative social institutions arise that meet these needs. In large
urban areas, where gay culture is more widely-developed, social groups
include athletic organizations that sponsor teams and tournaments;
leisure activity clubs in such areas as country-and-western dance, music,
yoga, bridge, hiking, and recreation; religious groups such as Dignity
(Roman Catholic), Integrity (Episcopal), and the Metropolitan Community Church (MCC); volunteer agencies such as information and crisis hotlines and charitable organizations; and professional and political
groups such as the Golden Gate Business Association of San Francisco
or the national lobby group, the Gay Rights Task Force. A directory
of groups and services is usually published in urban gay newspapers, and
their activities are reported on and promoted actively. Taken together,

these groups compose a culture that supports and nourishes a gay person's life.

GAY SYMBOLS

Gay culture is replete with symbols. These artifacts spring up and 15
constantly evolve as gayness moves from an individual, personal experience into a more complex public phenomenon. All groups express their ideas and values in symbols, and the gay culture, in spite of its relatively brief history, has been quite creative in symbol making.

The most visible category of symbols is in the semantics of gay 16
establishment names. Gay bars, bookstores, restaurants, and social groups want to be recognized and patronized by gay people, but they do not want to incur hostility from the general public. This was particularly true in the past when the threat of social consequences was greater. In earlier days, gay bars, the only major form of gay establishment, went by code words such as "blue" or "other"—the Blue Parrot, the Blue Goose, the Other Bar, and Another Place.

Since the liberalization of culture after the 1960s, semantics have 17
blossomed in gay place names. The general trend is still to identify the place as gay, either through affiliation (Our Place or His 'N' Hers), humor (the White Swallow or Uncle Charley's), high drama (the Elephant Walk or Backstreet), or sexual suggestion (Ripples, Cheeks, or Rocks). Lesbians and gay men differ in this aspect of their cultures. Lesbian place names often rely upon a more personal or classical referent (Amanda's Place or the Artemis Cafe), while hypermasculine referents are commonly used for gay male meeting places (the Ramrod, Ambush, Manhandlers, the Mine Shaft, the Stud, or Boots). Gay restaurants and nonpornographic bookstores usually reflect more subdued names, drawing upon cleverness or historical associations: Dos Hermanos, Women and Children First, Diana's, the Oscar Wilde Memorial Bookstore, and Walt Whitman Bookstore. More commonly, gay establishments employ general naming trends of location, ownership, or identification of product or service similar to their heterosexual counterparts. The increasing tendency of business to target and cater to gay markets strengthens the growth and diversity of gay culture.

A second set of gay symbols are those that serve as member- 18
recognition factors. In past ages such nonverbal cues were so popular as to become mythical: the arched eyebrow of Regency England, the green carnation of Oscar Wilde's day, and the "green shirt on Thursday" signal of mid-century America. A large repertoire of identifying

characteristics has arisen in recent years that serves the functions of recognizing other gay people and focusing on particular interests. In the more sexually promiscuous period of the 1970s, popular identifying symbols were a ring of keys worn on the belt, either left or right depending upon sexual passivity or aggressiveness, and the use of colored handkerchiefs in a rear pocket coded to desired types of sexual activity. Political sentiments are commonly expressed through buttons, such as the "No on 64" campaign against the LaRouche initiative in California in 1986. The pink triangle as a political symbol recalls the persecution and annihilation of gay people in Nazi Germany. The lambda symbol, an ancient Greek referent, conjures up classical images of gay freedom of expression. Stud earrings for men are gay symbols in some places, though such adornment has evolved and is widely used for the expression of general countercultural attitudes. The rainbow and the unicorn, mythical symbols associated with supernatural potency, also are common signals of gay enchantment, fairy magic, and spiritual uniqueness to the more "cosmic" elements of the gay community.

Another set of gay symbols to be aware of are the images of gay 19 people as portrayed in television, film, literature, and advertising. The general heterosexual culture controls these media forms to a large extent, and the representations of gay people in those media take on a straight set of expectations and assumptions. The results are stereotypes that often oversimplify gay people and their values and do not discriminate the subtleties of human variety in gay culture. Since these stereotypes are generally unattractive, they are often the target of protests by gay people. Various authors have addressed the problem of heterosexual bias in the areas of film and literature. As American culture gradually becomes more accepting of and tolerant toward gay people, these media representations become more realistic and sympathetic, but progress in this area is slow.

One hopeful development in the creation of positive gay role 20 models has been the rise of an active gay market for literature. Most large cities have bookstores that stock literature supportive of gay culture. A more positive image for gay people is created through gay characters, heroes, and stories that deal with the important issues of family, relationship, and social responsibility. This market is constantly threatened by harsh economic realities, however, and gay literature is not as well developed as it might be.

Advertising probably has done the most to popularize and inte- 21 grate gay symbols into American culture. Since money making is the goal of advertising, the use of gay symbols has advanced more rapidly

83

in ad media than in the arts. Widely quoted research suggests that gay people, particularly men, have large, disposable incomes, so they become popular target markets for various products: tobacco, body-care products, clothing, alcohol, entertainment, and consumer goods. Typical gay-directed advertising in these product areas includes appeals based upon male bonding, such as are common in tobacco and alcohol sales ads, which are attractive to both straight and gay men since they stimulate the bonding need that is a part of both cultures.

Within gay culture, advertising has made dramatic advances in the 22 past ten years, due to the rise of gay-related businesses and products. Gay advertising appears most obviously in media specifically directed at gay markets, such as gay magazines and newspapers, and in gay neighborhoods. Gay products and services are publicized with many of the same means as are their straight counterparts. Homoerotic art is widely used in clothing and body-care product ads. The male and female body are displayed for their physical and sexual appeal. This eroticizing of the body may be directed at either women or men as a desirable sexual object, and perhaps strikes at a subconscious homosexual potential in all people. Prominent elements of gay advertising are its use of sexuality and the central appeal of hypermasculinization. With the rise of sexual appeals in general advertising through double entendre, sexual punning, subliminal seduction, and erotic art work, it may be that gay advertising is only following suit in its emphasis on sexual appeals. Hugely muscled bodies and perfected masculine beauty adorn most advertising for gay products and services. Ads for greeting cards, billboards for travel service, bars, hotels, restaurants, and clothing stores tingle to the images of Hot 'N' Hunky Hamburgers, Hard On Leather, and the Brothel Hotel or its crosstown rival, the Anxious Arms. Some gay writers criticize this use of advertising as stereotyping and distorting of gay people, and certainly, misconceptions about the diversity in gay culture are more common than understanding. Gay people are far more average and normal than the images that appear in public media would suggest.

GAY MEETING BEHAVIOR

The final element of communication in the gay culture discussed 23 here is the vast set of behaviors by which gay people recognize and meet one another. In more sexually active days before the concern for AIDS, this type of behavior was commonly called cruising. Currently, promiscuous sexual behavior is far less common than it once was, and cruising has evolved into a more standard meeting behavior that helps identify potential relationship partners.

Gay people meet each other in various contexts: in public situations, in the workplace, in gay meeting places, and in the social contexts of friends and acquaintances. Within each context, a different set of behaviors is employed by which gay people recognize someone else as gay and determine the potential for establishing a relationship. These behaviors include such nonverbal signaling as frequency and length of interaction, posture, proximity, eye contact, eye movement and facial gestures, touch, affect displays, and paralinguistic signals. The constraints of each situation and the personal styles of the communicators create great differences in the effectiveness and ease with which these behaviors are displayed.

24

Cruising serves several purposes besides the recognition of other gay people. Most importantly, cruising is an expression of joy and pride in being gay. Through cruising, gay people communicate their openness and willingness to interact. Being gay is often compared to belonging to a universal—though invisible—fraternity or sorority. Gay people are generally friendly and open to meeting other gay people in social contexts because of the common experience of rejection and isolation they have had growing up. Cruising is the means by which gay people communicate their gayness and bridge the gap between stranger and new-found friend.

25

Cruising has become an integral part of gay culture because it is such a commonplace behavior. Without this interpersonal skill—and newcomers to gay life often complain of the lack of comfort or ease they have with cruising—a gay person can be at a distinct disadvantage in finding an easy path into the mainstream of gay culture. While cruising has a distinctly sexual overtone, the sexual subtext is often a symbolic charade. Often the goals of cruising are no more than friendship, companionship, or conversation. In this sense, cruising becomes more an art form or an entertainment. Much as the "art of conversation" was the convention of a more genteel cultural age, gay cruising is the commonly accepted vehicle of gay social interaction. The sexual element, however, transmitted by double meaning, clever punning, or blatant nonverbal signals, remains a part of cruising in even the most innocent of circumstances.

26

In earlier generations, a common stereotype of gay men focused on the use of exaggerated, dramatic, and effeminate body language—the "limp wrist" image. Also included in this negative image of gay people was cross-gender dressing, known as "drag," and a specialized, sex-

27

ually suggestive argot called "camp." Some gay people assumed these social roles because that was the picture of "what it meant to be gay," but by and large these role behaviors were overthrown by the gay liberation of the 1970s. Gay people became much less locked into these restraining stereotypes and developed a much broader means of social expression. Currently, no stereotypic behavior would adequately describe gay communication style—it is far too diverse and integrated into mainstream American culture. Cruising evolved from these earlier forms of communication, but as a quintessential gay behavior, cruising has replaced the bitchy camp of an earlier generation of gay people.

The unique factor in gay cruising, and the one that distinguishes   28
it from heterosexual cruising, is the level of practice and refinement the process receives. All cultural groups have means of introduction and meeting, recognition, assessment, and negotiation of a new relationship. In gay culture, however, the "courtship ritual" or friendship ritual of cruising is elaborately refined in its many variants and contexts. While straight people may use similar techniques in relationship formation and development, gay people are uniquely self-conscious in the centrality of these signals to the perpetuation of their culture. There is a sense of adventure and discovery in being "sexual outlaws," and cruising is the shared message of commitment to the gay life style.

CONCLUSION

These four communication elements of gay culture comprise only   29
a small part of what might be called gay culture. Other elements have been more widely discussed elsewhere: literature, the gay press, religion, politics, art, theater, and relationships. Gay culture is a marvelous and dynamic phenomenon, driven and buffeted by the energies of intense feeling and creative effort. Centuries of cultural repression that condemned gay people to disgrace and persecution have been turned upside down in a brief period of history. The results of this turbulence have the potential for either renaissance or cataclysm. The internalized fear and hatred of repression is balanced by the incredible joy and idealism of liberation. Through the celebration of its unique life style, gay culture promises to make a great contribution to the history of sexuality and to the rights of the individual. Whether it will fulfill this promise or succumb to the pressures that any creative attempt must face remains to be seen.

THE QUESTIONABLE VALUE OF FRATERNITIES

George D. Kuh,
Ernest T. Pascarella,
and Henry Wechsler

•

THIS SELECTION FOCUSES ON A specific kind of community with which you may have had direct experience—fraternities and sororities. After a period of decline during the sixties and seventies, fraternities and sororities have reasserted their presence on many college campuses. Along with their renewed popularity have come new controversies over alcohol abuse, date rape, and academic performance. This essay was written in April 1996 for The Chronicle of Higher Education, *a newspaper read by college professors and administrators. Education professors George D. Kuh and Ernest T. Pascarella, along with Henry Wechsler, the director of Harvard's College Alcohol Studies Program, take a critical view of fraternities and sororities and propose some reforms.*

For our analysis of identity and community, probably the most interesting issue discussed in the essay is how well fraternities and sororities create a sense of community for students. As you read the essay, you will see that supporters of the Greek system argue that the clubs play an important role in socializing freshmen and helping them feel as though they belong to a cohesive community. The authors, however, point out that although fraternities and sororities are "close-knit" and "supportive" to members, their membership is so homogeneous in terms of race, ethnicity, and sexual orientation that instead of bringing people together, they keep people apart. Consider, as you read and discuss this essay, how the author of the preceding essay, Randall E. Majors,

87

might respond to this criticism of fraternities and sororities. How have fra-
ternities and sororities contributed to the sense of community on your own
campus?

Almost monthly, a college or university fraternity makes the national news because of an escapade of underage drinking or a hazing episode resulting in bodily injury or worse. In fact, so many incidents of this sort occur that at least one law firm specializes in fraternity-related lawsuits. Such incidents tarnish the image of fraternities as a locus of brotherhood. 1

The response from fraternity leaders to those events is pre-dictable. With diverse memberships, they say, it is impossible for every-one to attain the high goals set by fraternities. Moreover, it's not just fraternity members who behave inappropriately, they note. Abuse of al-cohol is all too common among many students, whether they belong to a fraternity or not. Besides, proponents of fraternities assert, few other student organizations provide such an impressive array of bene-fits for their members and the host institution, benefits that far outweigh the occasional problems. 2

For example, fraternity leaders say, the grade-point averages of fraternity members on a campus sometimes exceed those of under-graduate men generally, evidence that fraternities contribute to aca-demic performance. And joining a fraternity helps newcomers adjust to college; without the experience of living in a close-knit, supportive group, many students would drop out. Fraternity life also helps give stu-dents a better understanding of people from different backgrounds, sup-porters say, and provides opportunities for leadership within the group that cannot be matched elsewhere on campus. As a result, they add, fra-ternity men and sorority women are disproportionately represented among community and professional leaders. 3

Unfortunately, many of these assertions are at odds with the re-sults of recent research. 4

While the majority of college students drink, fraternity members are much more likely than non-members to abuse alcohol, according to a recent study by the Harvard University School of Public Health. In surveying more than 17,000 students at 140 randomly selected four-year colleges, the study found that 86 per cent of those who live in fra-ternity houses were binge drinkers, compared with 45 per cent of non-members. 5

Particularly chilling but rarely mentioned is the large number of 6 sorority women who become binge drinkers. After they enter college, 80 per cent of the residents of sorority houses reported binge drinking, although only 35 per cent said they had binged in high school. Both fraternity and sorority members reported having more problems resulting from their drinking than non-members did. One example is unwanted sexual advances, reported by 43 per cent of sorority-house residents, compared with 23 per cent of non-members.

Alcohol abuse is only one area in which the performance of fraternity members falls far short of the espoused values and goals of fraternity life. Even though fraternities declare that academic performance is a high priority, during the orientation period new members' grades often fall well below the campus average. Many professors are convinced that the time-consuming, often inane activities required to pledge a fraternity are the primary cause; candid fraternity members agree. 7

Fraternity membership also has a negative influence on intellectual development. Data from the National Study of Student Learning, conducted at 18 four-year colleges by the National Center on Teaching, Learning, and Assessment, show that—even after controlling for initial differences in such factors as pre-college cognitive development, academic motivation, age, and selectivity of the college attended—fraternity men are well behind their non-member counterparts in cognitive development after the first year of college. The biggest deficit is in the area of critical thinking. The pattern is similar for sorority women, though the differences are not as pronounced as for men. 8

Personal development is affected, too. Although many fraternities attract people with varied academic and avocational interests, students encounter a broader spectrum of human differences in residence halls to which they are assigned randomly. In terms of race, ethnicity, and sexual orientation, fraternities tend to be more homogeneous than the student body in general. This is borne out by other data from the National Study of Student Learning. They show that, during the first year of college, fraternity and sorority members make significantly smaller gains than non-members do on measures of openness to diversity, which include valuing contact with people from different backgrounds and learning about people from different cultures. 9

The opportunity to develop leadership skills during fraternity life also may be overstated. Students gain competence in practical and interpersonal skills when they perform tasks requiring sustained effort and commitment, such as planning group and campuswide events. The majority of fraternity men do not hold positions, in their own group or elsewhere, that demand this kind of performance. Whether fraternity mem- 10 bers are overrepresented among contemporary business and community leaders is not known. And even if this was true in the past, in the future the fraternity experience may not be considered an advantage in one's career in civic leadership, given the disappointing findings related to fraternity membership and appreciation for human differences.

Supporters of fraternities surely will criticize this description of their educational impact. We readily concede that some individuals are unaffected by the anti-intellectual influences common to many chapters. And in some fraternities, alcohol abuse is not the norm, and high levels of intellectual and academic achievement are common. Unfortunately, research suggests that those fraternities are in the minority. 11

Reforming fraternities clearly is difficult. Even when the national officials of fraternities work with campus administrators to carry out new programs for recruiting and initiating members—programs that do not involve alcohol and hazing—the reform efforts often fail. Drinking and hazing are too deeply embedded in the cultural system of many chapters, where they are part of a complicated system of rewards and sanctions that bond the individual member to the group. 12

What is to be done? Colleges and universities need to assess how fraternities affect their educational missions, and to evaluate the political consequences of trying to change the deeply entrenched fraternity system. Generally, alumni have only fond memories of their fraternity and think it played an important part in their development and subsequent success. Campus administrators too often ignore the misdeeds of fraternity members because of the threat—direct or implied—that alumni will withhold their financial support. Therefore, before an institution undertakes any reforms, administrators must enlist the cooperation of all groups concerned and collect data related to the impact of fraternity membership on the educational development of students on that campus. 13

Most institutions would welcome assistance from the national offices of fraternities in designing reforms. But increasing the educational value of fraternities can be accomplished only campus by campus, using strategies specific to each institution. Campuses must delineate clear criteria that groups must meet for institutional recognition. Behavioral and educational standards must be set. Perhaps the best way to begin, after officials have assembled data showing the problems on their particular campus, is for the president to set up a blue-ribbon panel, headed by a top official such as the provost, to formulate strategies. The panel should include representatives of the faculty, student body, student-affairs staff, local fraternity leaders and members, 14 and alumni. Trustee support must be solicited. Fraternities that fail to cooperate should be ineligible for any form of institutional recognition, including the use of campus space for group functions.

Any attempt to reform the present system without convincing all   15
of the major players that change is necessary will surely fail. Even if reform succeeds — as seems to be happening in a few cases, such as at Colgate University — the most visible reformers can expect letters and public statements from fraternity alumni threatening to withdraw their financial support and challenging the reformers' loyalty to the institution. Such is the price of reclaiming the institution's educational integrity.

Because academic performance, intellectual development, and   16
openness to diversity seem to be negatively related to fraternity membership in the first year of college, policies barring first-year students from joining fraternities are essential. This is especially important on campuses where first-year students now can live in fraternity houses before classes begin; those institutions have little chance to socialize the newcomers to academic values. Deferring membership until the sophomore year also may make fraternity houses less rowdy, since fraternities may have strong economic incentive to make their houses more appealing to older members. Indeed, fraternity advisers report that many members now move out of the houses by their senior year, tired of the noise and drunken behavior of younger members.

Because many fraternities are indifferent to academic values and   17
seem to shortchange the education of many members, we need a careful examination of the educational benefits that fraternities provide. Colleges and universities must insure that fraternity members live up to the standards expected of all students and the standards that fraternities themselves espouse. When groups or individuals fail to meet these goals, administrators and fraternity leaders must act decisively to stem further abuse and reaffirm the institution's overarching educational mission.

PART II

WORK AND CAREER

*T*he readings in Part II encourage you to think about work and career—
your own hopes and fears as well as the problems and possibilities we face together
as a society. We begin with several readings that offer different perspectives about
work and career and that also relate these issues to the themes of identity and
community developed in Part I.

In "To Be of Use," poet Marge Piercy tells us that what she values most in
work is for it to be "real." In her opinion, "real" work enables the individual to
fulfill his or her sense of identity while providing an opportunity to be of use to
others. The next selection continues exploring the connections between work and
identity. "Finding Oneself through Work" by Robert N. Bellah and his team of
sociologists and philosophers explains three different conceptualizations people have
about their work—as a job, as a career, or as a calling. The authors point out that
these ways of thinking about work reflect what individuals value in their work as
well as in themselves as workers. The coming-of-age story, "How, Why to Get
Rich," by J. California Cooper tells what happens when a young African
American girl sets out to strike it rich. Alternately funny and sad, the story shows
how the girl's experience of working makes her alter her idea of the American
dream—giving up the fantasy of getting rich quick and recognizing what other
poor people are going through as they try to make a living.

The next three readings describe the current job market and how young
people about to enter it feel. "The Class of '96" by New York Times *business
reporter Kirk Johnson shows that college students today understand what they need
to do to get the best jobs and, if anything, are too caught up in planning their
careers. In contrast, economist-historian Neil Howe and satirist Bill Strauss argue
in "Chutes and (No) Ladders" that many young people today are passive and
unprepared, about to fall into an economic abyss. In "Getting Started: The Great
American Job Hunt," human resources and management professor Paul*

Osterman reports on research that helps explain why Johnson's college-age informants are optimistically planning for the future, while Howe and Strauss's teenagers are feeling more uncertain and undirected. He concludes by proposing that young people today need a "tech-prep" education to prepare them for jobs in the twenty-first century.

Next, we examine two snapshots of actual workplaces to see whether work today actually requires the special education that Osterman suggests. The first piece, "McDonald's—We Do It All for You" by Barbara Garson, describes what it is like to work at a high-tech fast-food restaurant. The second, "Working in Dilbert's World" by Steven Levy, describes what corporate life looks like through the eyes of Scott Adams's comic strip character Dilbert.

These readings contrast ideals about work and career with the reality for many workers and give us a sense of the problems that workers face. They are followed by a series of essays that analyze work and career problems and propose possible solutions.

The first is an essay by professor of management and economics Lester C. Thurow, who urges us to reexamine our assumptions about who is responsible for solving work and career problems. In "Survival-of-the-Fittest Capitalism," Thurow argues that if the American dream is ever to become a reality, we will have to put aside our typically American belief that individuals are responsible for their own success or failure. The essays that follow explore various ways other people, employers, and the government can help individuals solve these difficult work and career problems.

In "How the Maids Fought Back," Sara Mosle profiles members of the hotel employees union in Las Vegas to show how workers can help each other find solutions to their problems. Whereas Mosle writes about women in low-paying blue-collar jobs, Judith H. Dobrzynski in "Women on the Corporate Ladder" focuses on white-collar female executives who should be climbing the corporate ladder but seem to have been stopped by the glass ceiling. Her essay looks at some of the ways corporations have tried to help women advance in their careers.

Similarly, "Color Blind" by Ellis Cose examines corporate-sponsored affirmative action policies, specifically proposals to encourage racial diversity. Anthropologist Katherine S. Newman, in her proposal "Dead-End Jobs: A Way Out," is also concerned with what business can do to help employees. Focusing on the difficulty many inner-city fast-food workers have in finding better jobs, she makes a practical suggestion designed to benefit employees as well as their current and future employers.

Sociologist William Julius Wilson in "A Proposal for a WPA-Style Jobs Program" takes up Lester Thurow's challenge and argues that for one of the most serious problems—the lack of jobs for unskilled inner-city workers—the government has a role to play in providing solutions. He argues that we should

"Can Jennifer come out and work?"

Drawing by Cheney; © 1996 The New Yorker Magazine, Inc.

resurrect the WPA (Works Progress Administration), a public works program that was first instituted in 1935 as part of President Franklin D. Roosevelt's efforts to put America back to work after the Great Depression.

The final reading is a poem by Langston Hughes titled "Let America Be America Again." The poem passionately reminds us that the American dream is still only a dream and not a reality for the majority of Americans. Nevertheless, it ends on a hopeful note that we can overcome our problems and America can fulfill its destiny to become a true land of freedom and opportunity for all.

TO BE OF USE

Marge Piercy

∎

"TO BE OF USE" OFFERS a good starting point for thinking about work and career. It was written in 1972 by Marge Piercy, a novelist, essayist, and poet who was born in Detroit, Michigan, to working-class parents. (You can find another poem by Piercy, "Barbie Doll," in Part I.)

In this poem, Piercy says that what she values most is work that is "real." But what she means by real *is hard to define. As you read, consider what you value about work in relation to Piercy's values. In the first stanza, for example, you will see that Piercy describes the workers she admires as fully absorbed in what they are doing. Psychologists call this sense of absolute absorption a* flow state, *in which one forgets where one is and how much time is passing. If you have ever experienced a flow state, what was it like? Why do you suppose Piercy values it?*

Notice also how this poem invites us to think about work and career in terms of our sense of who we are as individuals and as community members. In the last two stanzas, Piercy suggests that "real" work offers us a way to express what is unique about ourselves. But it can be an important communal enterprise as well, a way for us to cooperate with and benefit others. When you think of your own career aspirations, do you think in terms of fulfilling yourself, of being useful, or do you think in different terms altogether?

The people I love the best
jump into work head first
without dallying in the shallows
and swim off with sure strokes almost out of sight.

They seem to become natives of that element,   5
the black sleek heads of seals
bouncing like half-submerged balls.

I love people who harness themselves, an ox to a heavy cart,
who pull like water buffalo, with massive patience,
who strain in the mud and the muck to move things forward,   10
who do what has to be done, again and again.

I want to be with people who submerge
in the task, who go into the fields to harvest
and work in a row and pass the bags along,
who stand in the line and haul in their places,   15
who are not parlor generals and field deserters
but move in a common rhythm
when the food must come in or the fire be put out.

The work of the world is common as mud.
Botched, it smears the hands, crumbles to dust.   20
But the thing worth doing well done
has a shape that satisfies, clean and evident.
Greek amphoras for wine or oil,
Hopi vases that held corn, are put in museums
but you know they were made to be used.   25
The pitcher cries for water to carry
and a person for work that is real.

FINDING ONESELF
THROUGH WORK

Robert N. Bellah, Richard Madsen, William M. Sullivan, Ann Swidler, and Steven M. Tipton

∎

THIS SELECTION COMES FROM Habits of the Heart: Individualism and Commitment in American Life *(1985), a book in which sociologists Robert N. Bellah and Richard Madsen collaborated with philosophers William M. Sullivan, Ann Swidler, and Steven M. Tipton to explain some of the traditions we use to make sense of ourselves and our society. As their title suggests, Bellah and his co-authors, like Piercy, are interested in understanding how we think about identity in relation to work and career.*

In "Finding Oneself through Work," the authors explain that people typically think of work as a "job," a "career," or a "calling." They also claim that each of these conceptions of work reflects and reinforces a particular self-image. For example, they argue that those who think of work primarily as a job tend to define and judge themselves in terms of the economic success and security they achieve. In what terms do you or your friends and family think of work? Which, if any, of these notions of work do you see in Piercy's poem or in any of the other selections you have read?

Consider also what Bellah and his team say about how our ideas about work are related to our sense of ourselves and our sense of community. To borrow Piercy's terms, what do you think makes work "real" to Bellah and his co-authors? What kind of work do they value and what do they value most about it? Contemplate what these or other views of work might imply about an individual's or a culture's beliefs and values.

The demand to "make something of yourself" through work   1
is one that Americans coming of age hear as often from themselves as
from others. It encompasses several different notions of work and of
how it bears on who we are. In the sense of a "job," work is a way of
making money and making a living. It supports a self defined by economic success, security, and all that money can buy. In the sense of a
"career," work traces one's progress through life by achievement and
advancement in an occupation. It yields a self defined by a broader
sort of success, which takes in social standing and prestige, and by a
sense of expanding power and competency that renders work itself a
source of self-esteem. In the strongest sense of a "calling," work con-
stitutes a practical ideal of activity and character that makes a person's
work morally inseparable from his or her life. It subsumes the self into
a community of disciplined practice and sound judgment whose activity has meaning and value in itself, not just in the output or profit
that results from it. But the calling not only links a person to his or
her fellow workers. A calling links a person to the larger community,
a whole in which the calling of each is a contribution to the good of
all. The Episcopal Book of Common Prayer says in the collect for
Labor Day, "So guide us in the work we do, that we may do it not for
the self alone, but for the common good." The calling is a crucial link
between the individual and the public world. Work in the sense of the
calling can never be merely private.

Though the idea of a calling is closely tied to the biblical and re-   2
publican strands in our tradition, it has become harder and harder to
understand as our society has become more complex and utilitarian and
expressive individualism more dominant. In the mid-nineteenth-
century small town, it was obvious that the work of each contributed
to the good of all, that work is a moral relationship between people, not
just a source of material or psychic rewards. But with the coming of
large-scale industrial society, it became more difficult to see work as a
contribution to the whole and easier to view it as a segmental, self-
interested activity. But though the idea of calling has become attenu-
ated and the largely private "job" and "career" have taken its place,
something of the notion of calling lingers on, not necessarily opposed
to, but in addition to, job and career. In a few economically marginal
but symbolically significant instances, we can still see what a calling is.
The ballet dancer, devoted to an ill-paid art, whose habits and practices,

beautiful in themselves, are handed down in a community based on a still-living tradition, so that the lives of the public may be enriched, is an example. In any case, however we define work, it is very close to our sense of self. What we "do" often translates to what we "are."

Each of our moral traditions carries a sense of the self at work distinguished by its peculiar idea of job, career, and calling in relation to one another.... To heed [the demand to make something of ourselves], middle-class Americans today leave home to go to school and then to work. For some, as for Margaret Oldham, what they learn in school leads smoothly into what they do in professional work. "Sometimes it feels like I've been a student all my life," she says of her dissertation research, "and when I finally finish, I'd still like to keep a hand in research and teaching besides seeing clients." But for most of those we talked to, as for Brian, school proved less a part of what they made of themselves at work. A self-described "under-achiever" in school, Brian majored in English at a midwestern state university, but devoted much of his time to parties, playing cards, and falling in love "at the drop of a skirt." English literature and the writing of romantic poetry were, however, among the things that brought him together with his first wife. After several years at a routine white-collar job to support his wife and a child, Brian returned to school for a semester of accounting courses, then entered the management training program of a major corporation. "I went in the Resources Management Program, which is made up mostly of graduates from engineering schools, mostly the top 10 percent of the class, and I finished number one in my class through that. Then I went into the Budget Office, which is made up of the top 1 percent of that group, and I finished in the top 1 percent of that group, so I figured, O.K. I can fit in that league, and I have proven that, so now let me go out and set about making a name for myself. In 1972 I was what they call on our rank structure rank four and in 1978 I was rank fourteen. My salary had increased three times over." Literary self-expression gave way to competitive self-advancement up the rungs of training "classes" set in a corporate ladder. Mastery of a discipline, for Brian, mattered less than finishing first in the class, since learning itself was chiefly a means of making it to the top of an organization structured by chains of supervisory control and salary scales.... 3

The high road to corporate success has led Brian back and forth across the country, "picking up, selling the house, moving off to a strange city and strange state" every few years, making new friends and then leaving them behind again. Even now, he is conscious of the next 4 step onward and upward: "I can probably make one more move locally. Beyond that I'd probably have to relocate geographically. Then I'd have to make a decision. Do I want the next level of challenges back East, or do I want to continue to enjoy the sunshine and lifestyle of California?"

Whatever his answer turns out to be, the forks in Brian's successful 5 career continue to dramatize the split between public and private life—between the challenges a public self takes on and the pleasures a private self enjoys. Yet work means more to Brian than the goods it buys and the status it secures. Most of all, it defines him in terms of his "performance" in comparison with others. "I don't like failure," he asserts. "I'm very competitive. I like to win." Finishing first among his corporate peers and leapfrogging from one promotion to another have brought Brian to the work he does today. He describes it as follows: "I am called a business manager. I have profit-and-loss responsibilities for a business that will do about fifty million dollars in sales this year. I have about sixty people that report to my staff, and prior to that I was finance manager for the department I'm in now." His responsibilities as a business manager extend from sales strategies to the bottom line of profits and loss, and no further. He defines his work by his corporate position, quantified in terms of gross revenue, profit margin, staff size, and span of control.

Still rising toward the peak of a career that has defined his iden- 6 tity by its progress, Brian looks back on his twenties and thirties, devoted to advancing his career at the expense of tending his marriage and family life, and concedes, "I got totally swept up in my own progress, in promotions and financial successes." Yet even now, Brian's definition of success revolves around an open-ended career on the upswing, empty of a calling's sense of social responsibility. "I want to keep progressing to the point where I remain challenged," he testifies. "Where I come as close as I can to performing at the absolute limits of my capability. That's success." That is also the voice of a utilitarian self seeking its separate identity in the exercise of its own growing powers, ever freer of restraint by others and ever farther out in front of them.

Midlife, especially for middle-class American men such as Brian, 7 often marks the "end of the dream" of a utilitarian self established by "becoming one's own man" and then "settling down" to progress in a career.[1] The grade grows steeper at the peak of a professional field, the ledges narrower at the top of a corporate pyramid. It becomes more difficult, or virtually impossible, to become "Number One"—sole owner-operator, chief executive officer, senior partner, or Nobel laureate. As these dreams die, the possibility fades of a self that can use work and its rewards to provide the matrix of its own transcendent identity. When the trajectory of a career flattens out, and it becomes clear that one will not, after all, make it to the top, then making it loses its meaning—as opposed to continuing in a calling and practicing law, carpentry, or scholarship as best one can, even if one cannot be the best. For many in middle age, the world of work then dims, and by extension so does the public world at large. For the fortunate among the career-weary, the private world of family and friends grows brighter, and a more expressive self comes to the fore.[2]

The alternative idea of work as a calling is conspicuously absent from Brian's pattern of success. Brian sees the value of work in terms of what it yields to a self that is separate from the actual activity work demands of him in return. In this imagery of exchange, the self stands apart from what it does, and its commitments remain calculated and contingent on the benefits they deliver. In a calling, by contrast, one gives oneself to learning and practicing activities that in turn define the self and enter into the shape of its character. Committing one's self to becoming a "good" carpenter, craftsman, doctor, scientist, or artist anchors the self within a community practicing carpentry, medicine, or art. It connects the self to those who teach, exemplify, and judge these skills. It ties us to still others whom they serve.[3]

Is the presence of a calling more evident in someone dedicated to an elite profession? Margaret Oldham, who finished at the top of her class all through college and won the chance to train as a clinical psychologist over hundreds of others, sees the personal meaning of her work from a different angle than does Brian. . . . Margaret chose psychology because of a desire to understand other people and why they were different from her. Here a self seeking to understand how we think and behave enters into a profession whose practical demands seem to strengthen personal identity. Yet academic research has turned out to be both enormously complex and artificially formalized, so that "usually by the time you get a really interesting question combed down into a research project, it's lost a lot of this complexity and stuff that made it interesting in the first place." Even when meaning is not lost in methodology, Margaret is "plagued by the idea that nothing I'm doing research-wise is ever going to have any relevance to anybody's life." The hope of becoming a person able to help others change their lives for the better guided Margaret toward a career as a therapist. But efforts to do so have all too often proved inconclusive, and sometimes simply hopeless, especially if their recipient was not "a YAVIS—young, anxious, verbal, intelligent, and sensitive." And, she adds, even "if you've done a really good job, they don't think you've helped them at all, and they think they've done it all themselves — and in a sense they have."

By most sociological measures, Margaret's work is much more re- 10
warding in terms of prestige and meaning than the work her parents do. Yet she asks much more *from* work and *for* herself than they do, she says, and that may be one reason she finds less "fulfillment" in work than they do. "Work is really what they do with their lives," she observes. "Working is what makes them feel worthwhile." She agrees with them that "people should work for what they get," and that "once you get into doing it, it kind of becomes an end in itself as well as a means to get your money or whatever it is that you want." But she does not fully share her parents' conviction that work is simply good and "what we're supposed to do." Nor does she always feel, as they seem to, that "work is a pleasure in itself." "I'm not as convinced of the all-importance of working as they are," she concludes. "It's important for me to do nothing sometimes, to relax," and so the big shift in her life is "doing more things for myself, taking more time for myself than I think that either one of my parents take for themselves. So to that extent I have succumbed to the 'me decade,' " she jokes, secure in the knowledge that compared to her peers the extent is minimal.

Compared to representative figures of our biblical and republi- 11
can past, however, Margaret is less than fully committed to her calling. She has not given up her dreams of clarifying the mind and making the world a better place, but she now wonders at times if psychology is "really the most fulfilling place for me to be." She looks back wistfully to the tangible creativity, discipline, and sense of completion she found in the pottery and craftwork she did as a student. Doing therapy does give her a sense of fulfillment: "Just the opportunity to get close to people in the way that you do in therapy is real nice and you grow a lot. You get better and better at sharing your emotions and giving to other people." But asked how therapy contributes to the larger social world or community, Margaret shakes her head and smiles ruefully, "The only community I ever think I'm adding to is the one of people who have been in therapy and talk like psychologists, you know, and that's not particularly positive."

For employed Americans, work offers not only the basis of a de- 12
cent material life but a great deal of self-esteem. Unemployment is peculiarly painful for those to whom what one does is what one is. Yet even for quite successful Americans, such as Brian Palmer and Margaret Oldham, work as job or career does not seem to be enough. To identify wholly with work in that sense is suffocating, even if the higher re-

wards are not limited by narrowing opportunities in the upper echelons. The absence of a sense of calling means an absence of a sense of moral meaning.

Notes

[1]See Daniel J. Levinson, *The Seasons of a Man's Life* (New York: Ballantine Books, 1978), chapters 13, 16, 18, 20; especially pp. 201–8, 245–51, 330–40. Compare George Vaillant, *Adaptation to Life* (Boston: Little, Brown, 1977), pp. 215–30.

[2]Gail Sheehy, *Passages: Predictable Crises of Adult Life* (New York: Bantam Books, 1977), chapter 20.

[3]See MacIntyre, *After Virtue* (South Bend, Ind.: University of Notre Dame Press, 1981), chapter 14.

How, Why to
Get Rich

J. California Cooper

．

This is a coming-of-age story about a girl and her get-rich-quick scheme. If you read the story in conjunction with the two preceding selections, you will observe that the girl's conception of work changes as she discovers what hard work really involves. Not only does she gain respect for people who do back-breaking labor day after day, but she also begins to see herself as part of a larger community with a social responsibility to help others improve their lives as she strives to improve her own.

If you agree that the girl changes in the course of the story, what do you think causes the change? She indicates at the end that she's doing a lot of thinking. How does her thinking about herself and others seem to be influenced by her experience picking onions? What do you think the American dream means to her? What does it mean to you?

In addition to short stories, J. California Cooper writes novels and plays, many of which have been performed on television and on the stage. Among her many awards are the James Baldwin Writing Award (1988) and the American Book Award (1989) for the collection of stories entitled A Piece of Mine. *"How, Why to Get Rich" is from another collection,* The Matter of Life, *originally published in 1991.*

You know, I'm just a kid, but I got nerves, and sometimes grown-up people just really get on em! Like always talkin about how kids don't have no sense "in these days." Like they got all the last sense there was to get. Everybody with some sense knows that if grown-up people had so much sense the whole world wouldn't be in the shape it's in today!

Cause don't nobody in the world seem to get along together, nowhere. Not even here, where they sposed to have most of the sense! 2

I came up, long with some war. It's so many wars you can't always remember which one. My mama and daddy moved to the big city to get rich workin at one of them shipyards. Gramma too. It was real exciting coming, drivin all cross the country of the United States. Coming to where the streets was paved with gold and all everybody was makin money. We was gonna save up a lot of it and go home. Change our lives, Daddy said. Get rich. 3

Well, we didn't get rich or nothing like it. We got changed, tho. We got a lot of other things, too. Like separated and divorced. Daddy met one of them ladies out from under one of them weldin hats was workin at the shipyard. And Mama was sweet-talked, or somethin, by somebody else was workin in the same shipyard! They sposed to be makin boats and ships and things down there and it look like they mostly made love and troubles, breakin up families! 4

Daddy's lady liked to party and stuff, so lotta our saving money went out that way. And him and Mama began to fuss and fight a lot, with Gramma runnin round sayin, "Now you all, now you all. . . ." But it didn't help nothin. 5

Then, Mama put him out and locked the door one night after he got off the "night shift." See, he really worked days. We had to move then, cause our money was cut in half or just even way down. 6

After while we moved into some cockroach's house. I don't know was it because of bein poor or nothin, maybe just cause it so crowded round here. Ain't hardly no place to rent near bout nice as our house what we was buyin back home what we left from to come out here and get rich. 7

Mama kept workin, naturally, and Gramma took to workin part-time domestic. It was just the three of us then, but things were high-priced and soon Gramma had to work full-time cause Daddy didn't bring no money much. 8

You could see everybody if you stayed out in the streets long enough, so I used to hang around places where he might be going to. Bars, gamblin shacks, Bar-B-Q shops. When I see him on the street he would always go in his pocket and give me some money, a big kiss and a hug. But not Mama. He wouldn't give her nothin, he said, cause she had a man-friend now. I didn't see no sense in that cause I was his child 9 and he was the only man-friend in my life. Help me! But he didn't, if I didn't catch him.

Gramma didn't like Mama's man-friend so, soon, Mama was 10
stayin away over to his room and it was just Gramma and me. Gramma tryin to work and make me a home so I'd be a good girl and grow up to be a good woman, and me tryin to catch my daddy on the streets with his bad woman for that extra five or ten dollars he would give me. This new place didn't have no streets paved with gold for us, but it sure did change our life. If I was a cussin person I could tell you what my Gramma says the streets are paved with!

Then, Gramma's other children who had come out here started 11
havin problems too. Either the mama or the daddy left and each one sent their children to live with us. With us! There was two, both boys.

Our life changed some more. Scuffelin round with Gramma on 12
what chores everybody else ought to do, who ate the most, got the dirtiest jobs and things like that. We all went to school. And we were poorer than ever. People sure can forget their kids! Just love em and leave em. They knew we had to eat and Gramma was workin hard as she could. We was poor. Government said we wasn't, but it sure felt like poor to us!

About this gettin rich, it's very easy to understand why anyone 13
wants to be rich. One big reason, for us, was we was poor, black and living in a ghetto. All three of us, my two fourteen-year-old boy cousins and thirteen-year-old me, were single children. That is we had one parent each . . . Gramma.

I will call one "John" (the slick one) and the other one "Doe" (the 14
kinda dumb one), and you can call me "Einstein" cause I was the smart one. Now Doe had come from the country, but John and me were from the city; leastways, a little city close to a big City. We always had the ideas, Doe was a hard worker, but very lazy at it.

Anyway, going on a paper route in the mornings (I went along to 15
manage things because my grandmother had to have absolute peace and quiet to sleep as late as she could before we helped her cook breakfast and she went to work), we always saw this gang of people on the street corner. Befuddled, dirty, poor-lookin, some winos, stuff like that, waiting for the bus to haul them to the country to pick fruit or something like that all day. Then they would be brought back to the same corner where they all began to stuff their hands in their pockets, hunch their shoulders and walk hurriedly away, kinda a tired hurry.

Now, we knew they must have made some money and were rush- 16 ing off to buy things with it! So, one morning I asked the bus driver how the job went, you know, how much and all? Well, he said fifteen cents a sack or a box depending on what was picked. That sounded pretty good to me when I thought of my two big strong cousins, so I asked what we had to do to get the job. The answer was to get a social security card and be on the corner at 5:00 A.M.

I thought about that for a week or so, then held a meeting and we all went down and lied and got our social security cards. I said I was twenty-six years old, so you know that was some government worker who wasn't thinking bout nothin cause she gave me my card and after my two cousins lied, gave em theirs, too! 17

We rushed home and explained everything to our grandmother, who listened and laughed a little when she told us that was hard work. Wellll, we know ALL work was hard to her so that didn't stop us! 18

She gave us some money to buy bologny and some other stuff after we arranged to pay her back. We fixed our lunches in the best happy mood we had been in, in a long time! We made a beautiful fat bologny sandwitch each and a piece of fruit; set them neatly in the refrigerator with our names printed neatly on each bag. We then went to bed to sleep, dreamin of all the money we were going to have! 19

I even counted up to maybe a year between the three of us and we could let me keep the money, some of it, save it and then maybe find a little business we could go into to get away from cockroach alley, the dirty looking characters and the winos round here. Set Gramma down. Not have to wait around waitin to catch my daddy. I had all our lives planned. I slept good that night! 20

Anyway, we woke up early, ate a little cold cereal, grabbed our lunches and rushed to the corner. Wellll, the bus was halfway down the block, leaving us! We screamed and hollored, but to no avail, cause he kept right on truckin. Oh! We were mad! And disgusted! After we got through blaming each other, we went home and got ready to eat our lunches when Gramma told us we better save em for the next day if we was gonna try again cause she wasn't buying no more! See? I knew I had to get rich! We sat the lunches in the refrigerator and went on out to get the papers we had stashed and deliver them to the people who almost didn't get them! 21

The next morning we skipped the cereal and rushed to the corner, but they were gone again! My Lord!! We were mad! We went home and put our lunches back in the frig. You know them sandwitches were beginning to turn up at the edges! Much less the fruit! We ate that 22 soggy fruit stuff on the way home in the dark morning. We hardly spoke for half a day or so . . . we all blamed each other.

The next morning, the THIRD one, we didn't even go to the bathroom or nothin. Went to bed dressed and ready and got up, grabbed them beat-out tired lunch bags and made it to the bus . . . on time. 23

Now, there was a very disgusting group we were goin with and we felt so superior to them mentally and physically. We knew we would be the champs that whole year and we laughed at them and everything! Especially one old lady who looked like she was 109 years old. 24

We just laughed at everything! We almost rolled in the aisle of the bus, but we kept it down except for that piece of laugh that sometimes busts out in spite of all you can do to hold it in! 25

One old wino-lookin man was telling everybody bout his experience as a picker and everything he said he would add, "Don't you know? Don't you know?" That cracked us up! We didn't listen to what he said, just how he said it. We found out later we shoulda just listened to what he was sayin. 26

Well, daylight was coming fast now, and the farther we drove, the hotter it was gettin to be. It didn't look hot, but when that big, ole red sun shone down on you through that ole dusty window, it was hot! The scenery was nice tho. You know, space and trees and a big sky and all. To a city kid, it was different. It was good. Like back home. I had forgot I missed it, with all the other stuff I had to have on my mind. We finally just relaxed and enjoyed it. I know it's some birds in the city, but we could SEE these, justa flying way out all over in the sky. The tall trees wavin and stretchin, like us, in the morning sun. And the sky . . . the sky was so clear . . . and blue. I got so relaxed and dreamy, I even dozed off a few times. Doe slept. John was still sniggling at the old wino til I told him to quit it cause he was nudging me with his elbow, lettin me know to listen to somethin and all I wanted, at that time, was to look out the dirty window and dream about stuff. 27

Anyway after bout two hours or so, the bus arrived at a field and we stretched quickly and flexed our muscles and jumped off. We were ready! Ready to get started on our big money! Everybody else just walked off, natural like. We grabbed two or three sacks each and told the man to point to our part. He said, "You all kin take any part but just stay in this section." Okey!! 28

It was an onion field. We started right in diggin and pullin them onions to load our sacks just like we was throwin money in them sacks. 29

We threw the extra sacks around our necks, but in two minutes that sun was so hot on our backs we threw them sacks off, watching where, so we would know how far we had to come back for them. We were organized!

Well, fifteen minutes later the bus driver came out and, waving his hands over his head, he hollered, "Wrong field, wrong field!" and pointed toward the bus to let us know to head back. Oh shit! we said to the sun (and we didn't even curse much usually). He continued, "Throw em down, leave em here!" We said to each other, "Not us! Hell, this is hard work!" Everybody else must have said the same thing cause everybody took a few onions out and threw them on the ground, then took their sacks on the bus with them. My cousin John, the city boy, grabbed all ours back when nobody was looking and some of the other ones too! He got on the bus with onions falling every-whichaway, saying they were all his.

Now, that onion smell . . . in that hot bus . . . was overpowering, so we were really glad to get to the right field. That took about ten minutes or so, then we were hopping out to get going again!

The sun wasn't even up very high, maybe it was about 9:30, but it was like it had been up there shining all week! I wanted to take some of my clothes off! But I'm a girl, and a lady, as my grandmama taught me, so I kept em on, even that thick cotton undershirt she had made me put on. Chile, I was hot!

We got started. The field was still onions. I stayed close to my cousins because the 109-year-old lady and I were the only two women and she didn't get no eye action, but the men seemed to look at me a lot from under their hats. See, I kinda had a little bust line, you know. So I was careful to stay close to protection should anybody lose their mind out there lookin at my new shape I was gettin! Anyway, now we could go to work for real.

Don't you ever let anyone tell you that an onion is smooth! You had to pull so hard to get them things out of the ground! My smooth, young skin started comin off on them onions. I went over to the bus man and asked for a knife to dig them with and he asked me, "How old are you?"

I lied, "Sixteen."

He said, "That ain't old enough, you have to be eighteen." He smiled with some yellow teeth between his cracked lips.

Darn! I hadn't lied enough! So I gave him a mean look and went on back to my row and my sack. I had about half a sack only. John and Doe were not too much further ahead of me, but everybody else was on their second row and their third or fourth bag! The 109-year-old lady even was workin on her third sack! Maybe she was only a hundred years old!

Well, anyway, at lunch time, two and a half hours later, I had a 38 bag and a half. John had two bags and Doe had about two and a half! I know John had stole some of them onions from the other sacks when he went to start a new row. At fifteen cents a sack, we had made ninety cents! Altogether.

Ach! (This picking was teaching me how to speak German.) We 39 only had three hours more to go and it was goin to cost us $1.25 each to pay for the bus trip! Ach! We hadn't asked Gramma for no money because that didn't make sense! WE were going to make plenty money! Besides, she would have screamed anyway. One, for waking her up, and two, for the money. The hundred-year-old lady had fifteen sacks. Fifteen! All by herself!

Lunch time. We got our lunch bags from the bus and looked for 40 some shade. Quick as we wipe the sweat away it would come right back. It was hot, hot, HOT! I have to say it three times! We were hot, sweaty and dirty and tired. Oh Lord, we was tired. My hands were raw. The sack was heavy and only half-filled. I had to lug mine with me everywhere just to keep my own cousins from takin any. We looked at each other and we almost cried! But . . . we were too strong for that. Besides, nobody wanted to be first to cry. We all knew one thing tho . . . we HAD to get enough onions to get home. That $1.25 each!

We opened our lunch bags (under no shade) and those bologny 41 sandwitches were almost rolls, they had turned up so far! The lettuce, an ugly shade of greenish-brown, we threw away. The tomato, we just sqwished and threw in the dirt (even the birds flew away from em). We ate at the rest.

Then a bean lunch truck drove up. Those beans were smelling 42 GOOD! All over that field! And we didn't have any money! Now . . . I knew enough to know that some of those men had been eyeing me all day and so I just walked over to the bean truck and stood there lookin like a hungry fool. My cousins just stood back and watched me. Somebody beckoned me to the bean window, but I shook my head with the saddest face I could make, I wasn't playin either, and said I didn't have any money. After a little while, the wino-lookin older man bought me a bowl of beans. A whole bowl of beans! Oh! they smelled so good! I smiled down at them and almost screamed with delight as I walked away from the man, thanking him. I even forgot how hot and tired I was. Only for a minute tho.

I had swallowed two mouthfulls when I felt the heat from the pep- 43
pers. The stuff was loaded with peppers! Flames seemed to, and did,
come out on my breath! I wished I was still starvin again. I gave the bowl
to my cousins who began to fight over it as I rushed to the water can!
I was still drinking water when they got there in a little while and
pushed me away from the water. Them beans was hot! Now we were
burning up on the outside from the sun and on the inside from the
beans. We were broke and had about six sacks between us! I went to sit
on the bus, mad, to try to think this out, since I am the one with the
brains. I snatched that paper contract we had signed, that the busman
gave me a copy of, from my pocket and started to read the fine print.
Could they leave us out there, God only knows where? If we didn't have
the dollar twenty-five each? You had to pay them when they paid you,
just before you left for home. Home. Oh, home, home, home. Oh,
Gramma, Gramma, sweet Mama, sweet Daddy. I woulda cried cept I
had to save my strength. But my heart felt like it was too big for my
chest, and it hurt to swallow.

My associates came on the bus to get the lowdown and I gave it 44
to them! We had to have the money. As we sat there, I looked out the
window and saw the old lady; she had bout eighteen sacks or more now.
That beat-up old lady! She had gone back to work early! She was taking care of her business. You know? I looked at that old lady and I respected her! I respected her because she was doing what she had to do
and she was doing it good!

I turned back to my problems cause I meant to solve em and re- 45
spect myself too.

I looked at my cousins . . . two of my problems! I told em where 46
we all stood. Doe, the country cousin, went back out there and really
started packing those onions. John, the city cousin, went out there to
see whose onions he could steal; his eyes darting back and forth over
the people in the field. My grandmama say you can just about tell who
is gonna go to jail in life, just by watchin what people do in their daily
livin. I began to understand her more. Then, I went to talk to the busman and show him my sore, raw hands, so I could get some sympathy
and maybe a free ride home, but he was busy, he said, so I got my sack
and started digging onions again, with tears in my eyes and evil in my
heart!

I don't know where they got that song from, "Shine On, Har- 47
vest MOON," cause I will never forget that sun shining on me in that
harvest. We really worked, tho. Doe was tryin to tear up those rows,
and John was stealin so fast that a man stopped him and musta told him

a few hard things that made him see the benefit of diggin his own onions cause he did work a few rows of his own for awhile. For awhile. No-body wanted to walk home after this hot, bone-tired day. We didn't talk, laugh or even smile anymore. Cause wasn't nothin funny no more.

Well . . . we got on the bus when it was time to go home. Some- 48 how we had made it! We had thirteen cents over the fare. Don't ask me how. Just thirteen cents, thats all. We sat with our mouths poked out all the way home. Thinking hard.

We had never really thought about labor and unions and all that 49 stuff. Or given too much attention to the civil rights movements, cause it didn't seem to touch us too much where we lived. But, now, we noticed there were not but two white people on the bus. All the rest of us were black, with a few mexicans, I guess, all colored in some way. But all poor, even the white ones.

I looked at that hundred-year-old lady who had worked so hard. 50 She might have been twenty years old for all I knew. Just tired and wore out, thats all! A hundred years worth of tired! My respect grew and something else I didn't know what to call it.

I tried to give the man who had bought the beans for me the thir- 51 teen cents, but he just shook his head, "No." Said, "Help somebody else on down the road someday." Then cracked his face into a kinda smile and waved me on away.

We were even too tired to doze off after we were crumbled in our 52 seats. We didn't see the trees and the sky on our way home. But I'm glad the space was out there . . . we needed it in that old, creaking, rattling, heaving bus that was hot and funky with the sweat of a hard day's "honest" work.

But there was something more . . . the smell of poor . . . the smell 53 of somebody's home being worse than those fields. Some had packed a few onions in their pockets or lunch bags. What, I wondered, would they buy with that body-breaking little money to go with those onions? I felt something . . . something . . . but I don't know what it was. It was just there in my mind.

My grandmama, even my mama, my daddy had done this kinda 54 work a little. I didn't want to talk about it. I just wanted to be quiet and feel it til I knew what it was. It felt a little like resignation . . . I seemed to catch it from the people in the bus. Something in me refused it. I changed it to indignation. For myself.

When we got off the bus at home, I knew why the people walked 55 hurriedly away. To rest . . . and forget, until tomorrow or . . . death, I guess. I don't know. I only know that day has made me think so hard. So hard.

We started home with the thirteen cents. Somehow, I started crying and they almost did, until we started laughing. Then we each took a penny and threw it in the street. Then we almost cried again from our aching bones, til we laughed again. We finally got home and told Gramma about it. She laughed so hard at us, we got mad at her and cried til we couldn't help laughing at each other.

She made us bathe. We didn't want to, we just wanted to fall out in the bed. After, we were glad we had washed all the onion, dirt and sweat off. Gramma gave us a good hot meal, store bought, then we hit that bed and I believe I was sleep midair on my way to the pillow. Gramma said we all snored like old men.

We always have to go to church every Sunday, whether we feel like it or not because Gramma says we have to learn what road to take in life. Nowwww, I understand what that means, a little better, cause I'm not takin that road out to them fields again! Not if I can help it! We like God too, I guess, because when we really couldn't think of what to spend that dime on and how hard we had worked for it, we decided to give it to Him. I don't know what the preacher did with it, but we gave it to God.

I don't know what John and Doe thought, but I said a prayer for that hundred-year-old lady, then for the man who bought the beans, then broke down and included them all. But the last thing I said to God was, "Please, please, don't let me make my life like that. Please."

Lately, I pay more attention to the labor and black movements. Or just poor people movements. Maybe I would be a labor official or something where you have some say bout what you do. I don't know. All I do know is I don't ever want to go pick nothing in no field no more unless it is my field, my own. Or I was the boss.

You know, you don't have to be white to be president of anything. Even of the United States. I could be president! Black as I am! And if you white and poor, you don't have to be rich to get to be president either.

I could be president! Even being a girl, a lady. Cause some of these laws and rules got to be changed!

I think about life too . . . my mama . . . my daddy. Maybe there is a reason or something for why they act like they do when they be working and tryin to make a livin. Separating and divorcin and all. They got to go out there and do it everyday! Work! I only did it for one day . . . and I was so tired and evil. I even cried, only for a minute tho.

Oh, I don't know. But I understand more what my grandmama is 64
tryin to teach me. I remember that hundred-year-old lady!

Yea. I think about all those things now. 65

I think I'm gonna hate onions for a long, long time, too. 66

And dumb boys. 67

Yes . . . I'm doing a lot of thinking. On how to get rich. Even just 68
how to make a real good livin for my life! Cause I already know why.

THE CLASS OF '96

Kirk Johnson

▪

KIRK JOHNSON, A BUSINESS REPORTER, originally wrote "The Class of '96" for a series of New York Times *articles about the state of the economy published in 1996 as a book called* The Downsizing of America. *Downsizing refers to the corporate mergers and reorganizations in the 80s and early 90s that led to thousands of white-collar managers and professionals losing their jobs. (Blue-collar factory workers have suffered most from earlier economic upheavals.)*

In "The Class of '96," Johnson profiles one group affected by downsizing— the present generation of college students. According to the people he interviewed, students now have more realistic career goals and begin earlier to prepare for the job market. As students become more focused, corporate recruiters increase the pressure to commit early to a career track. Companies are using internships, usually unpaid but credit-bearing work-study arrangements, to attract promising job candidates and give them some practical on-the-job training.

These trends may sound good, especially if you get an internship that leads to a job after graduation. But, as Johnson suggests, thinking too much about your future may turn your college education into vocational training rather than an opportunity to extend your knowledge. Similarly, if you are too careerist, you might not see work as a way of fulfilling yourself or being useful to others. Consider as you read whether these are issues that concern you and your classmates. If not, what other issues are of concern?

Ｉt may not really be necessary to scope out a life by the age of 21—it may even be counterproductive—but that hasn't made things any easier for Priscilla Stack. Ms. Stack is a bright, articulate psychology major from Mendham, New Jersey, who is distinctly lacking in focus. She doesn't know yet what she wants to do with her life, and in 1996, it would seem, that is a serious problem. There is pressure all around her, she complains, to choose and commit. It comes from friends, from parents, from potential employers, all of them beating the same maddening drum: competition is everywhere. You must dive in and start swimming. Stragglers lose. But, she wonders, what if you just don't know? And what if you choose wrong, plunging into a career only to find yourself trapped later in something you're really not very good at, or worse, that you hate? What if you wake up one morning in middle age and realize you messed up your life because of a decision you made in haste in your early twenties?

"Everyone has a direction," Ms. Stack said. "My dad is pounding on my head every time I talk to him. I feel like I have to make some kind of decision and pounce into it, but I just don't know." Even taking time off to grow up a little more . . . seems closed to her. Future employers, she said, might think her a slacker. "I know it's not good if you take time off after graduation," she said. "It doesn't look like you're very motivated." 2

For many students, pressures like that have profoundly changed the college experience. The old model of college as a heady intellectual adventure, they say, just does not make as much sense as it did a generation or two before. The sylvan images remain — studying under the broadleaf trees, stretching the boundaries of independence from parents — but the old view of college as a sheltered place to come of age, question assumptions, and find your own truth before embarking on real life is getting seriously squeezed. 3

"From what I see of the world in general, and especially for people my age, we're a little more realistic about our goals than our parents were," said Karim Abdul-Matin, a biology major from Brooklyn who is planning on a medical career in New York City. "We can't become anything we want anymore. We have a set number of options." Mr. Abdul-Matin has his own career track pointedly mapped out. He's intent on New York partly because that's where his family is, but also because he has connections there. Starting over in a new place is riskier now than it used to be, he believes, and any extra edge you can find must be used. He even knows where and how he wants to live: in a brownstone in the Park Slope section of Brooklyn. "The world is more established," he said. "There's not a sense of expansion the way there once was." 4

Professors who have seen the shift of generations say the pressure   5
to be practical or safe is so overwhelming that for many students, even
choosing a major has become an identity crisis: more than one in five
members of the class of 1996 is pursuing two degrees at once. "English
because they love it, economics to get a job," said Marilyn R. Mumford, who has taught English at Bucknell since the late 1950s. This
double-major trend, she said, is hardly a sign of confusion. "Students
today are much more self-conscious," she explained. "They have to ask
themselves more questions than the class of 1970 ever did, and I think
they have a better total picture of the role of education in their lives.
They have to keep their eye on the future." Professor Mumford wor-
ries, however, that by looking ahead so much, calculating the angles of
getting from point A to point B, the students are losing their appreciation of the here and now.

The changes in the economy have also altered political perspec-   6
tives. Douglas Candland, the psychology professor, says he sometimes
conducts a little experiment on the children of the 1990s: He starts talking about the Peace Corps. It sparks an argument every time, he said,
about the world and America's place in it.

The Peace Corps was one of the least complicated symbols of the   7
1960s. It spoke about youth and idealism, and the notion of improving
the collective condition of humanity. Today, Professor Candland said,
there are students in almost any class who will immediately attack the
Peace Corps as an agent of cultural imperialism. Who are we to say to
villagers in Africa or South America, the argument invariably goes, that
our way is better and that they should be like us?

To the class of 1996, America is just another player. Seniors are   8
more likely to talk about workers in, say, Singapore or China as tough
competitors than as objects worthy of compassion—never mind that
nations like China and Singapore aren't really the issue here. "It's not
a selfish generation, it's a scared generation," Professor Candland said.
"When you're worried about your own job or your parents' job, you're
just far less likely to be altruistic."

Corporate recruiters are helping to sharpen the focus on the here   9
and now. Over the last five years, career placement officials say, companies have dramatically stepped up their efforts, competing for the loy-
alties of students long before graduation. An executive at Andersen
Consulting, which has become one of the most aggressive of the new-
style recruiters, said the change in approach arose from the same cost-
cutting and efficiency pressures that drive the downsizing trend. According to Warren J. Dodge, a partner in the firm's New York office,

Andersen recruits at fewer colleges than it used to, but focuses on its chosen schools with a new intensity—grooming and developing potential employees beginning in their sophomore and freshman years, and, for promising minority candidates, even in high school. Mr. Dodge said Andersen tries not to pressure students. Other companies, he said, are the offenders. "We want to be recognized not as a recruiter, but as a partner," he said.

One senior who is ready to be a partner is Mike Wickerham, a 22-year-old management major from Pittsburgh with a giant American flag on his wall and a firm belief that capitalism is a struggle in which he will prevail. "I don't know where the country is going as a whole," he said. "But if there are only so many places, I'll have one of them."

Still, though, there are some rebels.

Alison Zampino would probably have more in common with the 1970 counterculture than with her own class. A psychology major from Belleville, New Jersey, with a pierced nose and a rough-edged style of dressing that owes nothing to J. Crew, Ms. Zampino said she would be going to San Francisco after graduation with no job and no particular goal except to live in a place that she has heard is nice. She will worry about making a living when she gets there. She has no commitments at this point in her life, and she likes the feeling.

But this is not 1970, and Ms. Zampino is constantly on the defensive about her decision. Some of her classmates suggest that she is lazy, or too rich to care, or cluck that she is wasting her life, throwing away her main chance. "They get this look," she said, "like, 'You just want to live?' "

CHUTES AND (NO) LADDERS

Neil Howe and
Bill Strauss

■

ECONOMIST-HISTORIAN NEIL HOWE AND BILL STRAUSS, *a political satirist who directs the comedy group Capitol Steps, have written two books:* Generations: The History of America's Future, 1584–2069 *(1991) and* 13th Gen: Abort, Retry, Ignore, Fail? *(1993), from which this selection is excerpted. The thirteenth generation (13ers, or generation X as it is often called) refers to people who were born between 1961 and 1981.*

The young people of this generation look quite different to Howe and Strauss than they do to Kirk Johnson in the preceding selection. Whereas Johnson describes them as too career oriented, Howe and Strauss represent them as basically passive and unprepared, perched on the edge of an economic abyss. While Howe and Strauss portray teenagers enjoying an affluent lifestyle, they also show the teens slaving away at after-school, low-paying, dead-end "McJobs." Although Howe and Strauss claim that this generation has "no illusions" about what the job market has to offer, they also suggest that young people are too caught up in the get-rich-quick version of the American dream to prepare themselves for the most rewarding kinds of jobs, those that require four or more years of college. Read "Chutes and (No) Ladders" in light of your own observation and experience, and then ask yourself whether Johnson or Howe and Strauss paints the more accurate picture.

TVs. VCRs. Boomboxes. Five-disk CD players. PCs hooked to speakers and stuffed with games. Porta-phones with caller ID and answering machines. Pushbutton remote controls lying around everywhere. That's the pop image of the 13er teenage bedroom, crowded like a movie-set condo with hi-tech amenities. During the day, that image rides to high school in convertible sports cars with space-age sound systems. On weekends, it lingers around the mall where 15-year-olds pull out credit cards to buy $100 Keds or $500 aviator jackets or $1,000 IBM clones with VGA color monitors. On prom nights, it rents a fortune in sleek clothes and travels by stretch limo. And when parents are away, it capitalizes on that magic moment (like the opening scene in *Risky Business*) when everything mom and dad own—five bedrooms, bar, luxury sedan, stuffed fridge, large-screen TV with HBO—becomes the personal fief of some teenage suburban prince.

The icons of 13er affluence reach well beyond their teen years. 2 Check out the student union of a large university: There it is, a minimall unimaginable twenty years ago, full of sports shops, restaurants, ice cream parlors, computer stores, fashion boutiques, banks, and travel agencies. Check out the juniors planning spring break: There they are, booking flights to Cancún and the Caribbean. Check out an inner-city crack house: There it is, full of young gangsters with gold chains and pocket beepers.

If older Americans have thus far shown little sympathy for the 3 13ers' economic plight, the reason lies largely in the sights and sounds of personal luxury that have surrounded 13ers since birth. Economic disease? Generational depression? How is that possible for kids whose teen bedrooms, college dorms, and gang houses are so decked out with lavish ornaments? Youth advertising, once reserved for cereal boxes or inside bubble gum wrappers, is now blazing away on prime-time TV, national newsweeklies, FM radio, public buses, rented videos, and highway billboards. Given that somebody's running all these ads—and given that what kids mostly buy are fancy shoes, pricey gadgets, and other discretionary stuff they want but don't really need—how could this generation be in such deep economic trouble?

Rarely does it occur to elders that juvenile wealth—what sociol- 4 ogist Jerald Bachman calls "premature affluence"—is in fact both a cause and a symptom of the 13ers' own impoverishment.

Much of this "premature affluence" is, of course, just image. Very 5 few 13ers really do cruise to school in Land Rovers or vacation in Bermuda. But the image has a force of its own. Corporate marketers, no longer prevented by law or social stigma from targeting today's "proto-adult" youngsters, hype the fantasy of high-living kids so that everyone (including disapproving elders) can't help but notice. Thirteeners reinforce the image with their own lifestyle attitudes. Sensing their own economic vulnerability, most prefer to idealize themselves as possessing the power and security and confidence they associate with wealth. Young people with cash tend to flaunt it. Those without much find ways to show off what little they have. To admit to poverty in circa-1990 America is to admit to all the individual incompetence, family ruin, and cultural dysfunction the public now associates with it.

Even where this affluence is real, moreover, the bustling youth economy masks four harsh truths about the 13ers' economic condition. First, much of it is not really "theirs" in the sense that it reflects any ability to provide for themselves. Instead, this 13er affluence is the mall and grocery shopping kids do for working moms and dads who don't have the time. Or it's the summer house-sitting kids do for globe-trotting neighbors. Or it's the cash or clothes or car that busy, well-off parents give their kids as a "reward" for time they have to spend alone. For reasons of convenience, elder Americans do leave a significant share of their national wealth to be handled, watched over, or wasted by dependent youths. But little of this wealth serves any long-term interest of the kids themselves — such as helping them to become future wealth producers. Instead, it can make teenagers feel like bored retainers milling around in some opulent palace, having momentary, hopeless fun with whatever baubles the Rajah leaves lying around. 6

True, 13er teens do earn a vast amount of money (over $60 billion a year) from their own jobs. In fact, theirs is the biggest child labor generation since the days of turn-of-the-century newsboys and garment girls. The high school students of the '80s and '90s are working longer hours for pay (after school and during summers) than any previous generation of high-schoolers in American history. Yet the second harsh truth is that all this labor represents, in life cycle terms, a miserable return on youth energy and youth time. The typical teen job is a low-skill service slot offering little training and no chance for advancement, generating nothing but short-term cash. And once that cash is gone, the countless hours that might have been invested in skilled training or academic study are gone forever. The traditional youth jobs that once prepared earlier youth generations for adult careers — in farms, family-owned businesses, skilled crafts, heavy industry — have mostly vanished. Instead, the typical teenage 13er can work her heart out for years and still find herself no more employable than the day she started. 7

Third, the earnings of dependent youths ordinarily buy a level of affluence that still reflects a massive parental subsidy. In most American homes, after all, these earnings are linked to a perverse quid pro quo: Parents, wanting their kids to learn the value of money and become self-reliant individuals, typically allow them to do whatever they 8 want with whatever they make. Thirteeners are thus far less likely than prior generations to help pay for their own room and board or to help fund their own future education and training. Bearing few living expenses and not expected to save, a generation of teenagers has become accustomed to a subsidized level of consumption they could not possibly afford on their own. Once in college, many continue to cultivate expensive tastes—the safe and secluded dorm, the squash court, the dessert tray—oblivious to the real estate nightmare and Hamburger Helper that await them after graduation.

The fourth harsh fact about youth affluence is that it's strictly temporary: It comes with a Cinderella clock. Usually, crunch time comes soon after a 13er leaves home or leaves school. This is the period, say opinion surveys, when today's young adults start getting dissatisfied with their living standards. College loans shift from payout to payback time, at rates of interest way above the three percent charged Boomers back in the '60s. Child support payments dry up from divorced dads. Dentists and doctors have to be paid with wallet cash. Jobs take longer than expected to land. Salaries are painfully small, especially by the standard of the prematurely affluent teen's own inflated expectations. 9

How small? To begin with, take a look at polls showing that most teenagers (of both sexes) expect to earn $30,000 or more by age 30. Then, take a look at Census surveys reporting what American men age 25 through 29 really earn. In 1990, there were *eight* with total annual incomes of under $30,000 for every one making over that amount. (And there were fifty making less than $15,000 for every one making over $75,000.) Even these earnings don't go as far as many 13ers once imagined they would. Money that used to go toward the discretionary consumer goods of a leisured lifestyle now has to go into rent, food, commuting, and other necessities—if it can stretch that far. . . . 10

Thirteeners entering the labor market have no illusions that the system welcomes what they have to offer. Experience at part-time after-school jobs? Forget it. Unskilled labor puts cash in their pockets, but two of every three 13ers consider it useless as a stepping-stone to later employment. High school degree? Maybe that's enough, if your mom owns the store or your uncle's a union steward, or if you don't mind competing in the global wage market against nimble fingers in Bangladesh. Apprenticeships? Shyeeaah riiight, provided you can still find one of the 3,500 slots available across the entire United States. Armed forces? Great for a couple years, but then what? The big heroes of Desert Storm got laid off, and the Cold War's over. College degree? That doesn't impress big corporate employers like it once did. Profes- 11 sional degree? Maybe, but good luck breaking into a partnership full of older careerists with oversized egos, endless credentials, and nowhere else to go. Today's economy offers its biggest rewards to an aging class of winners whom economist Robert Reich calls "symbolic analysts" and offers the least to everybody else. By preparation and reputation, 13ers understand that they fall into the "everybody else" category.

Most . . . typically end up with the low-wage keyboard, phone, 12 counter, delivery, and cleaning jobs Boomers have always found demeaning: the service-sector "McJobs" that sociologist Amitai Etzioni describes as "more time-consuming, less character building" than what talented youths used to expect. Even here, the typical 13er attitude is to wait for a break, prove themselves, and squeeze their way up, from cashier to stock clerk to night manager. They're especially attracted to working arrangements (dealer franchises, sales commissions, piecework, temping, and performance bonuses) that reward initiative and offer at least some hope of striking it big. They devour rags-to-riches stories wherever they can find them—like the one about the thousand 13er programmers at Microsoft's Seattle-area headquarters who've become stock-option millionaires. . . .

So this generation finds itself playing not *Monopoly*, but a real-life 13 game of *Chutes and* (No) *Ladders*. Facing the economic future, each 13er finds himself essentially alone, to an extent that most elders would have difficulty comprehending. Between his own relative poverty and the affluence he desires, he sees no intermediary signposts, no sure, step-by-step path along which society will help him, urge him, congratulate him. Instead, all he sees is an enormous chasm, with him on one side and everything he wants sitting on the other.

GETTING STARTED: THE GREAT AMERICAN JOB HUNT

Paul Osterman

∎

THIS ESSAY'S ANALYSIS OF EMPLOYMENT statistics helps explain why Kirk Johnson paints a rosier picture than do Howe and Strauss. The difference is education, according to professor of human resources and management Paul Osterman. College graduates are not only more likely to get jobs, but the jobs they get are more likely to pay well and to offer opportunities for advancement and creativity. The people most in danger of falling into the abyss Howe and Strauss describe are high school dropouts, especially African Americans and Latinos who have a significantly harder time finding employment than do their Anglo counterparts.

Written in 1994 for the Wilson Quarterly, *this essay follows up on Osterman's earlier research published in* Getting Started: The Youth Labor Market *(1980) and* A National Policy for Workplace Training *(1993). In addition to helping us understand the problems facing young people today, Osterman turns our attention to possible solutions. Consider, for example, whether Germany's system of tracking students would be feasible here or whether it would undermine the American dream (if not the reality) of equal opportunity. Why do you suppose Osterman emphasizes that the new "tech-prep" education he proposes include "serious" academic subjects as well as training for the skills employers are requiring?*

We live in an age of anxiety about jobs, and perhaps the greatest anxiety is felt by young people searching for their first employment. All the other dangers and discontents of the world of work—from stagnant wages to insecurity bred by corporate "re-engineering"—

seem to form a dark ceiling over those who are putting their feet on the lowest rungs of the ladder. Not only must today's young endure a larger-than-usual share of the uncertainties of starting out, but they must contemplate a future that seems truncated and unpromising. The news media have cast them as an "edgy," cynical, and disheartened "Generation X," the first generation in American history, we are constantly told, that cannot look forward to a future better than its parents had. A staple of the Generation X story is the young person who invested in four years of college and yet finds himself in a job well below what he expected, both in terms of what it demands and what it pays. The *Washington Post* tells of college graduates forced to take unpaid internships because real jobs are unavailable. *Time* says it all in a headline: "Bellboys with B.A.'s."

There is a crisis among young people who are trying to get started in life, but it is not quite the crisis that the news media describe and its causes are not quite what one might expect. The facts simply do not support a terribly gloomy view of the immediate prospects for the middle-class, college-educated kids who are generally labeled Generation X. It is true that wage growth, an important part of the escalator of upward mobility, has slowed or ended, and it is far from certain that the old more-or-less automatic increases will resume. College-educated men aged 25 to 29, for example, earned an average of $28,963 in 1992, roughly the same amount in real dollars as in 1983. (Their female peers, however, improved their earnings by a bit more than 10 percent.) But while average pay may not have increased, college grads still get good jobs, jobs that give them responsibility, decent pay, room for a little creativity, and opportunities for advancement. In the boom years of 1984–86, about 47 percent of newly hired college grads in their twenties landed jobs in top-shelf occupations, as executives, managers, or professionals. The years 1989–91 saw a slight decline, to 45 percent, but this hardly represents a collapse of the job market. And another 40 percent of the 1989–91 crowd landed jobs in other desirable areas: technical work, sales, and administration, including jobs as various as air traffic controller, cashier, stockbroker, and ticket and reservations agent.

Slow economic growth has increased the risks facing college graduates and ratcheted up their anxiety. On university campuses a more somber career-oriented atmosphere prevails, shocking the visiting journalists who came of age in sunnier and, some would say, dreamier days. It takes more time and more effort to get a good job, and often the pay is disappointing. Nonetheless these young people are still in relatively good shape.

The young people who face true difficulty are those with less education. They are in fact the great majority of young jobseekers. In 1992, only 23 percent of 25- to 29-year-olds had a college degree. Another 48 percent had some college or an associate's degree. Sixteen percent had only a high school diploma, and 13 percent lacked even that. In the past, there was a fairly reliable route that kids without college could follow. After high school and perhaps a year or two of college, they churned through a succession of less-than-desirable jobs before settling down. Instead of learning job skills in school, they went through an extended period of what economists call "labor market adjustment." They might work a string of jobs as retail clerks, construction workers, or unskilled factory hands, punctuated by short spells of more-or-less voluntary unemployment. Then, as now, many twentysomethings were not ready for permanent jobs. They were mainly interested in earning some spending money for an apartment and a car and, perhaps, in having a little fun with their coworkers on the job. Few cared much what kind of job it was. 4

With age, maturity, and new family responsibilities later in their twenties, these people settled down into "adult jobs," but the paths they followed were many and varied. Credentials were less important than personal contacts, and many found their adult jobs through the help of parents, relatives, and friends. The young man who followed his father into a particular factory or mine might not have been typical, but his informal way of getting started was. Uncle Bob might pull some strings for you at the union hall or Mom's best friend might tip you off to an opening in the billing office. This system, if it can be called that, succeeded for most people because jobs were plentiful and because most of the skills workers needed could be learned on the job. Today many young men and women cannot count on either the old routes or the old destinations. The factory likely is silent, the union hall half empty, and the help-wanted ads full of jobs requiring specialized skills. Ready to make the leap into adulthood, these young people find there is no obvious place to land. 5

The system still works for large numbers of high school graduates; most move gradually from "youth jobs" to "adult jobs." The National Longitudinal Survey of Youth, which followed a group of young people between 1979 and 1988, offers a sharper picture of the problem areas. It found that 44 percent of 16- to 19-year-olds worked in wholesale or retail trade, which offers mostly low-paying and high-turnover 6 positions. But by ages 20 to 31 the fraction employed in this sector was down to only 17 percent. Moreover, the study shows steadily growing work commitment among the young people. Only 3.5 percent of the oldest men in the study and four percent of the oldest women were unemployed at the time of the last interview. All of this suggests that the process of integrating the young into the workplace is going fairly well. Yet one also needs to know whether the jobs are steady and whether people are enjoying long stretches without unemployment. Here the news is more troubling. Among employed 29- to 31-year-old high school graduates who did not go to college, more than 30 percent had not been in their position for even a year. Another 12 percent had only one year of tenure. The pattern was much the same for women who had remained in the labor force for the four years prior to the survey. These are adults who, for a variety of reasons—a lack of skills, training, or disposition—have not managed to secure "adult" jobs.

For blacks and Latinos, the malfunctioning of the job market has reached a critical stage. In 1993, only 50 percent of young blacks between the ages of 16 and 24 who were not in school even had jobs. Among young Latinos the figure was 59 percent. By contrast, nearly three-quarters of their white counterparts had jobs. (A college degree significantly narrows but does not close the gaps. Ninety percent of white college graduates in the age group were employed, as were 82 percent of the black graduates and 85 percent of the Latinos.) 7

Young people in many other industrialized countries have a lot more help getting started. In Germany, virtually all students except the small number bound for universities spend the last three years of high school in an apprenticeship system that combines part-time schooling with training in factories, labs, and offices. For each of some 400 recognized occupations there is a standardized curriculum that specifies the skills to be taught on the job and the content of schooling. The system is overseen by committees of representatives from government, business, and unions. After formal examinations at the end of high school, new graduates are placed in "adult" jobs, often with the company that trained them. 8

Not all German apprentices can find employment in their field; the Germans, a notoriously well-fed people, joke that they always seem somehow to turn out too many bakers. Yet inculcating the essentials of workplace behavior—be prompt, dress properly, follow instructions—is nearly as important a function of the system as teaching particular skills. The German system has other drawbacks. Women are still "gen- 9 der tracked" into fields such as hairdressing, and the system can be slow to react to technological change in the workplace. Still the training and placement help German youngsters receive are far superior to what is available to their American peers.

In Japan, the process of launching the young into the world of 10 work is not so highly organized as it is in Germany, but it is still far more structured than in the United States. Teachers maintain contacts with employers and play an important role in placing high school graduates. In Japan, as in Germany, the first job is a giant step into the work world. The years of casual, American-style "job shopping" are virtually unknown in these countries, and especially in Japan the young are expected to remain with their first employer for a long time. Yet if the American system is less orderly, it also provides much more freedom for the individual to experiment and change his or her mind — highly prized qualities that should not be lost in any attempt at reform.

Finding a steady job is only half the challenge of getting started. 11 Finding one that pays relatively well is the second, and lately most daunting, hurdle. Pay for college graduates has at least stayed even over the years, but high school graduates and (especially) dropouts have lost a lot of ground. There now exists a huge pay gap between the college educated and their less fortunate peers. Between 1979 and 1991, the real wages of high school dropouts fell more than 20 percent, and the wages of high school graduates without college degrees fell more than 11 percent. People equipped with only a high school degree are finding it increasingly difficult to earn a decent living. According to a recent U.S. Census Bureau report, nearly half of all 18- to 24-year-olds who worked full time in 1992 still had annual incomes below $14,335, the poverty line for a family of four.

The labor market is sending a clear signal. While the American 12 way of moving youngsters from high school to the labor market may be imperfect, the chief problem is that, for many, even getting a job no longer guarantees a decent standard of living. More than ever, getting ahead, or even keeping up, means staying in school longer.

While many things may have contributed to the erosion of wages 13 over the past two decades, including the oft-cited influxes of cheap immigrant labor and cheap imported goods, the new premium on skills explains much of what has happened. When new technologies are combined with new ways of organizing work, such as team production or total quality management programs, the need for various kinds of skills rises. Today, employees are asked to understand and analyze certain kinds of data, to think about ways to improve the processes and prod-

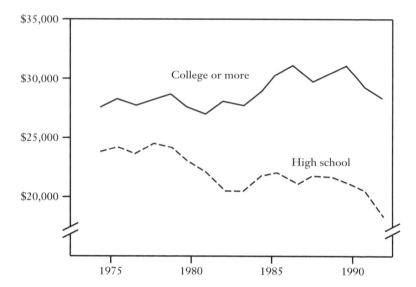

A Tale of Two Degrees (Annual Earnings of Men Aged 25 to 29, by Education, in Constant Dollars)

SOURCE: Housing and Household Economic Statistics Division, U.S. Bureau of the Census

ucts of the workplace, and to work with others to bring improvements about. No longer is it enough to perform rote tasks on an assembly line.

In part, employers are looking for better command of "hard" skills such as math, and the best evidence for this is the fact that they are willing to pay for such hard skills with hard cash. Economists Richard Murnane, John Willett, and Frank Levy recently found that, six years after graduation, members of the high school class of 1986 who had scored in the top third of a standardized math test were earning 16 percent more than those who had scored in the bottom third. In the class of '72, by contrast, top scorers enjoyed an edge of only five percent six years after graduation.

This is a graphic illustration of the growth in demand for relatively simple math skills. And they are "relatively simple." Skills of this sort are not out of reach for most people. The question is whether the schools can do a good job of providing them. The answer is a little more textured than the bitter criticisms of political leaders and employers suggest. In fact, there is little reason to believe that schools are providing worse training than in the past. Scores on the National Assessment of Educational Progress, which declined during the 1970s, generally rose during the 1980s. Kids in most age groups scored slightly higher on most tests at the end of the '80s than they did in the early '70s. High school dropout rates have even improved a bit: In 1972, 16.1 percent of 19- to 20-year-olds lacked a high school diploma and were not enrolled in school. By 1991, that number was down to only 14.3 percent.

The real problem appears to be that jobs (and employers) are requiring ever-higher levels of skill, and that the schools, though moving slowly forward, are failing to keep up. Test scores have not declined, but they are not very impressive either. The National Assessment of Educational Progress, for example, offers the depressing claim that 30 percent of young people lack basic literacy skills (e.g., the ability to collect information from different parts of a document) and that 44 percent of 17-year-olds cannot compute with decimals, fractions, and percentages. And while it is nice that dropout rates are not rising, they are still too high, especially among minority groups: 17 percent of young blacks and 36 percent of Latinos are dropouts. 16

Employers, moreover, are not simply looking for technical skills. The workplace of the 1990s, with its team-oriented approach and quality programs, requires people who are able to work cooperatively with others. They need good interpersonal skills. The same is true in the service sector—from fast-food restaurants to airlines—where there is a growing emphasis on pleasing the customer. When asked in a survey conducted by the National Association of Manufacturers why they rejected job applicants (more than one reason could be given), 37 percent of employers cited writing skills and 27 percent cited math skills, but 64 percent cited ability to adapt to the workplace. 17

Thus, despite all the talk of a "deskilled" nation of hamburger flippers, the American labor market is demanding more and more skill. Although unskilled service-sector work has certainly grown, so has the quantity of more demanding work. Indeed, the U.S. Bureau of Labor Statistics projects that between now and 2005 the occupational group with the fastest growth rate will be "professional specialty" jobs—such as engineering, the health-care professions, and teaching—almost all of which require at least some college. Growth in executive, administrative, managerial, and technical occupations will also be faster than average. 18

It is important for those who would fix the American system to put aside utopian thoughts. Getting started will always be a difficult, 19 anxiety-producing experience. Moreover, young people are and will continue to be marginalized in virtually every labor market in the world. Even Germany does this, albeit subtly, by placing them mostly in apprenticeships at small firms, where long-term career prospects are not good. Young people simply lack the skills and maturity of their elders, and in any event it makes sense to reserve most good jobs for people with adult responsibilities.

Hearkening to the German example, American policymakers have 20 focused on the need to strengthen links between local schools and employers. The Clinton administration's new School to Work Opportunities Act, budgeted at $100 million this year, encourages employers to provide on-the-job training and encourages schools to reformulate their curricula to include real-world examples that can be used both to motivate and to teach. The new "tech-prep" education, unlike the old vocational education, seeks to give teenagers serious instruction in traditional academic disciplines. The hope is that by appealing to a bigger slice of the teenage population, the low-prestige, second-rate taint of old-fashioned vocational education will be avoided. Making all of this work in the highly decentralized American system will be difficult. Individual school systems must be persuaded to rethink how material is taught. Without strong European-style employers' associations, there has to be firm-by-firm recruitment of "good" employers to train students and hire graduates. Still, the effort is well worth making.

Ultimately, however, helping the young find good jobs is more 21 than a matter of tinkering with what happens to teenagers in school and on the job. One of the top requirements in today's job market is schooling beyond high school. This means that increased financial aid to help more youngsters attend college must be a high priority. Likewise, the employment problems of black and Latino youngsters owe much to a daunting array of larger urban ills, from crime to inferior education, for which narrowly focused programs—with the exception of the tiny Job Corps—have been unable to compensate. Overcoming this group's special problems will require large helpings of collective as well as individual ambition and initiative.

MCDONALD'S— WE DO IT ALL FOR YOU

Barbara Garson

■

THIS SELECTION FROM BARBARA GARSON'S *book*, The Elecronic Sweatshop: How Computers Are Transforming the Office of the Future into
the Factory of the Past *(1989), calls into question Paul Osterman's theory
that young Americans need a special education to prepare them for today's high-
tech workplace. Garson also wrote* All the Livelong Day: The Meaning and
Demeaning of Routine Work *(1975; rev. ed. 1994) and various novels and
plays including the political satire* Macbird *(1966).*

*"McDonald's—We Do It All for You" gives a snapshot of what it is
like to work at a high-tech fast-food restaurant. The technology has probably
changed since the late 1980s when Garson's informant Jason Pratt worked
there, but it is likely that the corporate ethos or spirit has remained pretty much
the same. Jason's description of the work he does at McDonald's reinforces the
idea suggested in Garson's book title that today's high-tech workplace is an
"electronic sweatshop," a factory where assembly-line workers are little more
than cogs in a machine. You may be surprised that Garson uses the term*
sweatshop *to describe McDonald's. What connotations does the word have
for you?*

*Based on your own experience and observation, what do you think peo-
ple need to learn in high school or college to succeed in such a job? Consider also
what people can learn from working at a place like McDonald's. Recall what
Amitai Etzioni (quoted in Howe and Strauss) says about "McJobs" being "less
character building" than you might expect. What, if anything, do you think
sales or fast-food jobs can teach teenagers that would help them in their future
careers?*

133

"They called us the Green Machine," says Jason Pratt, recently retired McDonald's griddleman, " 'cause the crew had green uniforms then. And that's what it is, a machine. You don't have to know how to cook, you don't have to know how to think. There's a procedure for everything and you just follow the procedures." 1

"Like?" I asked. I was interviewing Jason in the Pizza Hut across from his old McDonald's. 2

"Like, uh," the wiry teenager searched for a way to describe the all-encompassing procedures. "O.K., we'll start you off on something simple. You're on the ten-in-one grill, ten patties in a pound. Your basic burger. The guy on the bin calls, 'Six hamburgers.' So you lay your six pieces of meat on the grill and set the timer." Before my eyes Jason conjures up the gleaming, mechanized McDonald's kitchen. "Beep-beep, beep-beep, beep-beep. That's the beeper to sear 'em. It goes off in twenty seconds. Sup, sup, sup, sup, sup, sup." He presses each of the six patties down on the sizzling grill with an imaginary silver disk. "Now you turn off the sear beeper, put the buns in the oven, set the oven timer and then the next beeper is to turn the meat. This one goes beep-beep-beep, beep-beep-beep. So you turn your patties, and then you drop your re-cons on the meat, t-con, t-con, t-con." Here Jason takes two imaginary handfuls of reconstituted onions out of water and sets them out, two blops at a time, on top of the six patties he's arranged in two neat rows on our grill. "Now the bun oven buzzes [there are over a half dozen different timers with distinct beeps and buzzes in a McDonald's kitchen]. This one turns itself off when you open the oven door so you just take out your crowns, line 'em up and give 'em each a squirt of mustard and a squirt of ketchup." With mustard in his right hand and ketchup in his left, Jason wields the dispensers like a pair of six-shooters up and down the lines of buns. Each dispenser has two triggers. One fires the premeasured squirt for ten-in-ones—the second is set for quarter-pounders. 3

"Now," says Jason, slowing down, "now you get to put on the pickles. Two if they're regular, three if they're small. That's the creative part. Then the lettuce, then you ask for a cheese count ('cheese on four please'). Finally the last beep goes off and you lay your burger on the crowns." 4

"On the *crown* of the buns?" I ask, unable to visualize. "On top?" 5

"Yeah, you dress 'em upside down. Put 'em in the box upside down too. They flip 'em over when they serve 'em." 6

"Oh, I think I see." 7

"Then scoop up the heels [the bun bottoms] which are on top of 8
the bun warmer, take the heels with one hand and push the tray out from
underneath and they land (plip) one on each burger, right on top of the
re-cons, neat and perfect. [The official time allotted by Hamburger
Central, the McDonald's headquarters in Oak Brook, Illinois, is ninety
seconds to prepare and serve a burger.] It's like I told you. The procedures makes the burgers. You don't have to know a thing."

McDonald's employs 500,000 teenagers at any one time. Most don't 9
stay long. About 8 million Americans—7 per cent of our labor force—
have worked at McDonald's and moved on.[1] Jason is not a typical ex-
employee. In fact, Jason is a legend among the teenagers at the three
McDonald's outlets in his suburban area. It seems he was so fast at the
griddle (or maybe just fast talking) that he'd been taken back three
times by two different managers after quitting.

But Jason became a real legend in his last stint at McDonald's. 10
He'd been sent out the back door with the garbage, but instead of coming back in he got into a car with two friends and just drove away. That's
the part the local teenagers love to tell. "No fight with the manager or
anything . . . just drove away and never came back. . . . I don't think
they'd give him a job again."

"I would never go back to McDonald's," says Jason. "Not even as a man- 11
ager." Jason is enrolled at the local junior college. "I'd like to run a real
restaurant someday, but I'm taking data processing to fall back on." He's
had many part-time jobs, the highest-paid at a hospital ($4.00 an hour),
but that didn't last, and now dishwashing (at the $3.35 minimum).
"Same as McDonald's. But I would never go back there. You're a complete robot."

"It seems like you can improvise a little with the onions," I sug- 12
gested. "They're not premeasured." Indeed, the reconstituted onion
shreds grabbed out of a container by the unscientific-looking wet handful struck me as oddly out of character in the McDonald's kitchen.

"There's supposed to be twelve onion bits per patty," Jason in- 13
formed me. "They spot check."

"Oh come on." 14

"You think I'm kiddin'. They lift your heels and they say, 'You 15
got too many onions.' It's portion control."

"Is there any freedom anywhere in the process?" I asked. 16

"Lettuce. They'll leave you alone as long as it's neat." 17

"So lettuce is freedom; pickles is judgment?"   18

"Yeah but you don't have time to play around with your pickles.   19
They're never gonna say just six pickles except on the disk. [Each store
has video disks to train the crew for each of about twenty work stations,
like fries, register, lobby, quarter-pounder grill.] What you'll hear in
real life is 'twelve and six on a turn-lay.' The first number is your hamburgers, the second is your Big Macs. On a turn-lay means you lay the
first twelve, then you put down the second batch after you turn the first.
So you got twenty-four burgers on the grill, in shifts. It's what they call
a production mode. And remember you also got your fillets, your
McNuggets. . . ."

"Wait, slow down." By then I was losing track of the patties on   20
our imaginary grill. "I don't understand this turn-lay thing."

"Don't worry, you don't have to understand. You follow the beep-   21
ers, you follow the buzzers and you turn your meat as fast as you can.
It's like I told you, to work at McDonald's you don't need a face, you
don't need a brain. You need to have two hands and two legs and move
'em as fast as you can. That's the whole system. I wouldn't go back there
again for anything." . . .

Listening to [Jason] made me remember what Ray Kroc had written   22
about his own job (head of the corporation) and computers:

> We have a computer in Oak Brook that is designed to make real estate   23
> surveys. But those printouts are of no use to me. After we find a promis-
> ing location, I drive around it in a car, go into the corner saloon and the
> neighborhood supermarket. I mingle with the people and observe their
> comings and goings. That tells me what I need to know about how a Mc-
> Donald's store would do there."[2]

By combining twentieth-century computer technology with   24
nineteenth-century time-and-motion studies, the McDonald's corporation has broken the jobs of griddleman, waitress, cashier and even
manager down into small, simple steps. Historically these have been service jobs involving a lot of flexibility and personal flair. But the corporation has systematically extracted the decision-making elements from
filling french fry boxes or scheduling staff. They've siphoned the know-
how from the employees into the programs. They relentlessly weed out
all variables that might make it necessary to make a decision at the store
level, whether on pickles or on cleaning procedures.

It's interesting and understandable that Ray Kroc refused to work   25
that way. The real estate computer may be as reliable as the fry vat

probe. But as head of the company Kroc didn't have to surrender to it. He'd let the computer juggle all the demographic variables, but in the end Ray Kroc would decide, intuitively, where to put the next store.

[Jason] would like to work that way, too. So would . . . [other Mc-₂₆ Donald's employees like] June and Damita. If they had a chance to use some skill or intuition at their own levels, they'd not only feel more alive, they'd also be treated with more consideration. It's job organization, not malice, that allows (almost requires) McDonald's workers to be handled like paper plates. They feel disposable because they are.

Notes

[1]These statistics come from John F. Love, *McDonald's Behind the Golden Arches* (New York: Bantam, 1986). Additional background information in this chapter comes from Ray Kroc and Robert Anderson, *Grinding It Out* (Chicago: Contemporary Books, 1977), and Max Boas and Steve Chain, *Big Mac* (New York: Dutton, 1976).

[2]Ray Kroc and Robert Anderson, *Grinding It Out* (Chicago: Contemporary Books, 1977), p. 176.

WORKING IN
DILBERT'S WORLD

Steven Levy

■

"WORKING IN DILBERT'S WORLD" SHOWS us another American workplace — the white-collar, corporate office that Newsweek *business and technology editor Steven Levy calls an "air-conditioned sweatshop." Levy, who has also written several books including* Hackers: Heroes of the Computer Revolution *(1984) and* Insanely Great: The Life and Time of Macintosh, the Computer That Changed Everything *(1994), wrote this essay for* Newsweek *magazine in August 1996.*

Although "Dilbert" is a satiric comic strip, Levy tells us it offers a realistic portrait of contemporary corporate culture. He cites one management expert who calls it a "documentary," and he attributes much of its enormous popularity to the fact that office workers recognize the problems it satirizes as real problems they face every day.

Like the "McJobs" Garson describes in the preceding reading, many of the problems Dilbert satirizes seem to be caused or at least exacerbated by too great an emphasis on productivity, which requires that fewer workers do more work in less time. To enhance productivity, for example, workers are often discouraged from using their imagination and taking the initiative, actions that could not only make work more satisfying but also increase productivity. Why do you think productivity is so important? What other goals do you think employers should promote?

Is it real . . . or is it "Dilbert"?

(A) A software engineer, recently refused a promotion, is receiving his performance review. He asks the boss why he got passed over.

"You're not a team player," says the boss. "What do you mean I'm not a team player?" asks the stunned employee. The answer: "You didn't smile in the company photo."

(B) A boss and a subordinate are traveling together on a business trip. At an airport layover, the subordinate goes to a pay phone to check the office voice mail for messages. The boss appears fascinated. "You mean," he says, "you can check voice mail while you're on the road?"

(C) A consultant brought in by the brass addresses a group of managers and engineers at a meeting. To improve the company's business processes, he says, "I'll show you how a well-designed process can compensate for your sloth, apathy and all-around incompetence." There is a deadly pause. Then the consultant adds, "But most important—let's have fun."

The answers to this quiz, which you are probably taking at your desk instead of the work that your soulless boss thinks you're doing, are (A) real life (it happened to a programmer at a brokerage firm); (B) real life (the experience of a marketing manager at a Fortune 100 firm), and (C) "Dilbert." The last, of course, is the title of a daily comic strip that has suddenly won its own promotion from cult status to mass phenomenon. Its creator is Scott Adams . . . , himself a former middle-managed cubicle dweller.

But you probably know this. You also probably have one or two "Dilbert" strips push-pinned to the wall of your own 9-by-9 slice of the workplace. You devour the strip daily in one of the 1,100 newspapers that run it, you purchase the "Dilbert" books that have assaulted the best-seller charts ("The Dilbert Principle" has topped the *New York Times* list), and your mouseclicks may well contribute to the 1.5 million hits that The Dilbert Zone Web site accumulates daily. One thing is unmistakably clear to the hordes who compulsively follow the fortunes of the strip's eponymous hero, a mouthless engineer with a perpetually bent necktie: the bedrock truth of the American workplace, at least in the white-collar corporate caverns where clerks, engineers, marketers and salespeople dwell, is not to be found in the heaving stacks of business books in the local Barnes & Noble, nor in the neatly bound reports of the McKinseys and other management-consulting firms. It's in the comics. In fact, the blithely clueless remark by the consultant cited in (C) may well have been uttered in some bland conference room by a real person, and reported to Scott Adams in one of the 300 or so e-mail messages he receives in an average day.

That's why your score on our little quiz really doesn't matter.

(That's right, another pointless workplace exercise.) The contrast between "Dilbert" and real life is . . . almost nonexistent.

"It's not a comic strip, it's a documentary—it provides the best   8
window into the reality of corporate life that I've ever seen," says Mike Hammer, author of "Reengineering the Corporation," who is a fan despite the fact that Adams often lampoons his theories. Another management expert, Guy Kawasaki of Apple Computer, agrees. "There are only two kinds of companies," he says. "Those that recognize they're just like 'Dilbert,' and those that are also like 'Dilbert' but don't know it yet."

If this is true, woe betide us all. The workplace according to "Dil-   9
bert" owes less to Edward Deming or Tom Peters than to George Orwell and Franz Kafka. The title character is a nerdy loser toiling in a constricting cubicle. He can't get respect or a date. His dog, the potato-shaped Dogbert, is a cheerful yet ruthless consultant, whose not-terribly secret goal is to rule the world and enslave all humans. Catbert is a human-resources director who before distributing pink slips toys with employees as if they were balls of yarn. The only one with a modicum of wisdom is the garbage collector, who has cleverly opted out of the system.

The central tenet of this dyspeptic corporate vision is the Dilbert   10
Principle. As Adams put it, "The most ineffective workers are systematically moved to the place where they can do the least damage: management." Of course, this creates maximum damage, as their idiocy permeates corporate life. "It seems as if we've turned nature's rules upside down," Adams writes. "We systematically identify and promote people who have the least skills."

Every month or so in the "Dilbert" workplace, some bizarre man-   11
agement fad dribbles down to the drones: Reengineering, Total Quality Management or paintball tournaments. They are time-wasters at best, tortures at worst. Hours are spent in meetings about deadlines, deadlines that get harder to make because of all the hours spent in meetings. Technology has run amok; the engineers understand how it works, but the bosses—who can't tell the difference between a Power-Book and an Etch-A-Sketch—don't get it at all. Every so often, an order comes from above to devote massive amounts of time to make everything "ISO9000 compliant"; no one knows what ISO9000 is. Instead of getting products out the door, people are asked to memorize mission statements. And in the background, burning ever closer, are the fires of Competition, triggering the dread drums of Downsizing. "Knock knock," says the boss. "Who's there?" asks the employee. The boss grins: "Not you anymore!"

Dilbert® by Scott Adams. Reprinted by permission of United Features Syndicate, Inc.

If this isn't hell, it's close. Even "Dilbert's" creator admits that those two tufts of hair sticking out of the boss's mostly bald pate are modeled on the Devil's horns. "Over time," says Adams, "his personality gets more defective, and his horns get higher, making him look even more demonic."

Are things really that bad in real life? Are we all as doomed as Dilbert, destined to pass out from exhaustion from working in air-conditioned sweatshops? Stephen Roach, chief economist at Morgan Stanley, seems to admit as much when he says downsizing, wage stagnation and a shortsighted corporate efficiency mania have drastically changed the work environment to the detriment of the worker. "It has certainly raised questions of cynicism, loyalty, perceived sense of worth and career aspirations," he says, neatly summarizing the traumas at Dilbert's unnamed yet universal employer. On the other hand, surveys show that a lot of us are fairly satisfied with our jobs. A Newsweek Poll conducted this summer indicated an impressive majority—87 percent—considered their workplace a "pleasant environment."

Dilbert® by Scott Adams. Reprinted by permission of United Features Syndicate, Inc.

So why is everyone reading "Dilbert" and saying, "Hey, that's my   14
job"? Scott Adams has a theory: "If you're in an absurd situation and
you're not changing it, then you define it as being OK," he says. "Most
people say, 'My job is good, but today I had a really bad time'." It's anal-
ogous to the way people view Congress. Overwhelmingly they will register disapproval—and then go out and reelect their own representative. When the pollsters zeroed in on the details, it turned out that the
workers indeed are living in "Dilbert's" world. More than 70 percent
experience stress at work. When asked whether unnecessary rules and
red tape prevent them from doing their best job, half agree. The biggest
complaint seems to be poor communication between management and
workers—64 percent claimed that this impeded their work. And there's
no confidence that good work alone will reap rewards: when asked
what gets someone promoted, people were equally divided between how
good a job one does and how politically connected one is.

What the survey does not show is the suppressed rage of workers   15
who tolerate abuses and absurdities in a marketplace leaned-and-
meaned to Wall Street's specifications. Reading "Dilbert" allows them,
in some small way, to strike back, or at least to experience a pleasant
catharsis by identifying the nature of the beast: a general yet pervasive
sense of idiocy in corporate America that is seldom dealt with by the
captains of industry who have great hair and offices with doors. Here
is a sampling of phenomena where the comic strip is uncomfortably
close to real life:

Cubicles. A former cubicle dweller himself, Scott Adams has   16
made Dilbert's dinky domain a prime symbol of workplace humiliation.
There are companies, such as chipmaker Intel, where everybody, even
the CEO, works out of a warren. But generally, dispatching someone
to one of those pasteboard waffle holes is a public, self-fulfilling
prophecy of subpar performance. "If you put somebody in a cubicle,"
says Adams, "you cannot expect him to make decisions which are higher
quality than cubicle decisions."

Adams has gotten mileage out of other so-called alternative of-   17
fice strategies like Hoteling (spaces are divvied out daily, first come, first
served), Shared Space (employees confined like two-to-a-cell prison-
ers) and Free-Address (workers share large, open, hivelike spaces). The
newest horror among the boxed set is "densification," when employers
literally close in the walls on the workers to save floor space. "It's part
of a constant nickel-and-diming of the employee," says Adams. " 'I
want you to work another hour—and make the cubicle two feet
smaller'."

Bad Bosses. While boss-hating is an honored tradition, in the   18
'90s there's more reason for it than ever. "With downsizing and cost
containment, the pressure on bosses has increased in remarkable ways,
and instead of kicking the dog, they often kick the subordinate—and
those people often kick their subordinates," says Harvey Hornstein, a
psychologist and author of "Brutal Bosses." No wonder some of the
most popular "Dilbert" strips are the ones where the superior torments
his underlings, like the one where he offers to raise an employee ap-
praisal if the worker eats a bug. ("It's way more motivational if I pick
the bug," says the boss.) It's not hard, however, to find real-life tales
that top the transgressions in the comic strip. There's even a Web site
devoted to such horror stories—www.myboss.com.

Or just listen to a former worker at an East Coast high-tech com-   19
pany where the president walked around the office turning down the
air conditioning, even though employees worked in hot, windowless offices. "People were literally sweating on their desks," says the worker.

Management Fads. "In the '50s and '60s, management heretics   20
espoused that participation, egalitarianism and involvement would not
just make people happier, but improve the bottom line," says Art
Kleiner, author of "The Age of Heretics: Heroes, Outlaws, and the
Forerunners of Corporate Change." Sounds great, but then the Dilbert
Principle kicked in, and the programs came under the control of idiots.
Mishandled and forced upon workers, these schemes now succeed only
in making workers more cynical—and less productive. Typical is the
middle manager at a financial-services firm, living under the boot of one
of the ubiquitous total-quality programs: "Paying attention to customers and quality is what I do every day," he says, "but now I have to
hang up signs and post measurements."

Out-of-Control Technology. Technology does enhance the   21
workplace: it boosts productivity, it distributes all-important information around the company, it enables workers to play solitaire without
shuffling cards. It also makes bosses look even more clueless than usual,
like the executive at a government regulatory agency whose answer to
every technological dilemma is "get a bigger disk drive." For some reason, though, the bosses wind up with the snazziest computers, which
gather dust while underlings struggle with wheezing old boxes that
can't run Windows 95.

Too Much Time at Work. Ever since Apple's Macintosh de-   22
velopment team in the mid-1980s wore T shirts proclaiming 90 HOURS
A WEEK AND LOVING IT! high-tech companies have figured out it's good
business to coax triple-time work out of single-salary employees, and

the practice seems to have spread to other sectors of the workplace. But Americans don't love spending all their time at work—40 percent of NEWSWEEK'S Poll respondents think their employers ask too much of them. Dilbert's boss, for instance, thinks nothing of drawing a time line for a project that has the hapless engineer designing "a client-server architecture for our worldwide operations"—in six minutes.

An indication of how far this has gone is one of the latest corporate trends: "home-at-work." The idea is that since employees are being asked to spend almost all their waking hours at the office, the least the company can do is let them entertain themselves with the computer. So the company permits them to do banking, personal e-mail and even recreational Net-surfing at their workstations. Meanwhile, the main contact these drones have with their families is by viewing snapshots of their kids on the World Wide Web. 23

Downsizing. In Dilbert's company, it's done by Dogbert's "can-o-matic," a device disguised as a toilet that "randomly fires people by slapping a pink slip on their backs and catapulting them out of the building." But whether it's done to lower costs, impress Wall Street and get rid of that chimerical deadwood, downsizing is the defining reality of the workplace today. If everybody weren't so worried about being Dogberted, the absurdities of the workplace would be infinitely more tolerable—and the "Dilbert" strip would be shorn of its sharpest edge. 24

Dilbert® by Scott Adams. Reprinted by permission of United Features Syndicate, Inc.

Surprisingly, Scott Adams himself thinks that downsizing does make the workplace more efficient—fewer workers means less time to waste on idiotic pursuits like vision statements, meetings and reorganizations. What gives Adams grist for the "Dilbert" mill is the way managers mishandle downsizing, not only in the often cruel manner in 25 which the news is broken, but in its sometimes counterproductive effects. Nynex, for instance, has shed thousands of employees since 1990. Union rules protect senior workers, "but our younger employees were the ones who had taken more time to educate themselves," says a remaining technician. "We have actually gotten rid of our best people." This practice — of getting rid of the brightest workers — happens so often that it has its own term: brightsizing.

Corporate Double Talk. Why don't managers say what they really mean? Because then you'd know. "My boss actually said to me, 'Let's bubble back up to the surface and smell the numbers'," marvels Toph Whitmore, an analyst at a software firm in Bellevue, Wash. "I had no idea what it meant." 26

At worst, business communication is purposely misleading. "My company put out a memo that told us to go home over the July Fourth weekend and relax," says an engineer at a Silicon Valley firm. In fact, the firm was mandating the workers to use vacation days for the long weekend — something that the employees understood immediately. All this, of course, leads to cynicism and resentment. Sometimes it's little things that put workers over the edge — like the company that declared that engineers using the whiteboard would be limited to two marker colors. Other times it's bigger things, like seeing workers blown away like props on the "Twister" set. As a result, the American workplace nods in agreement at the "Dilbert" cartoon where the boss admits that he was mistaken when he previously claimed that "employees are our most valuable asset." Actually, he explains, they're ninth. Eighth place? "Carbon paper," says the boss. 27

Is there any hope that the workplace can improve? A number of consultants think so, and cite the strip itself as an antidote to corporate mindlessness. Adams himself has hopes that his comic strip may actually change the problems that he satirizes. "Somebody told me that their company now has a Dilbertization committee," he says. "The idea is to find things their company does that could potentially be fodder for a 'Dilbert' cartoon strip, and change it. This is repeating itself in other companies. It almost seems like there are fewer absurdities happening." 28

There's a problem with that theory, though. In order for the strip to have those effects, the bosses first have to Get It. According to the Dilbert Principle, this will happen around the same time that cubicles learn to fly. Consider the small but telling event that occurred recently at a Midwestern company. A manager went over to a worker's desk and noticed a "Dilbert" posted on the wall. In the strip, the boss was com- 29 plaining that a report was too readable. Could Dilbert muddy up the language a bit? "Oh," the manager chuckled, "isn't that the truth?" Then she changed the subject—after reviewing a document for the seventh time, she wanted the worker to redo it yet again.

Real life . . . or "Dilbert"? Hard to say. The only difference is that with "Dilbert," it doesn't hurt so much when you laugh. 30

SURVIVAL-OF-THE-FITTEST CAPITALISM

Lester C. Thurow

■

In this essay, professor of management and economics Lester C. Thurow urges us to think about who is responsible for solving work and career problems. Thurow has written many articles and books, including The Future of Capitalism: How Today's Economic Forces Shape Tomorrow's World *(1996). Most of the readings in Part II suggest that individuals need to alter their perspective or gain new skills. The Levy piece on "Dilbert," goes even further, implying that workers can do little to improve an inherently absurd system. In "Survival-of-the-Fittest Capitalism," which first appeared in January 1996 in the* Los Angeles Times, *Thurow argues that we can find workable solutions if we would only view work and career problems as social and political rather than personal.*

Look closely at Thurow's argument that Americans typically regard these problems as personal because we believe that individuals are responsible for their own success or failure. Consider whether you agree that this belief in individual responsibility is quintessentially American. Is it, for example, part of the American dream or the Protestant work ethic?

Thurow takes this belief in individual responsibility to the extreme when he argues that it is leading us from "laissez-faire" capitalism (which strictly limits government interference in the lives of individuals) to "survival-of-the-fittest" capitalism (which leaves individuals to solve their own problems, without government help). Whether or not you agree that we are in danger of sliding down the slippery slope Thurow warns about, you may believe that individuals alone cannot solve problems of inequity in the system. If so, who else do you think should help find and implement solutions?

147

Everywhere in the wealthy industrial world, governments are 1
facing enormous economic pressures. Global competition from equally
skilled but lower-waged workers in the Second and Third worlds pushes
wages down. A skill-intensive shift in technology is creating a group of
low-skilled First World citizens who cannot earn First World wages.
Expenditures explode as governments try to finance the generous pensions and health care that the elderly have come to expect. Tax revenue
lags far behind because of the slow growth that central banks impose
to fight inflation.

While the economic pressures are identical, different social and 2
cultural institutions and different political attitudes are producing very
different effects within the wealthy industrial world. In the United
States, real wages have fallen for 80% of the work force and the corporate sector has massively downsized. In the public sector, both President Clinton and the Republican majority in Congress are proposing
large cuts in the social welfare system with only minor disagreements
about how large these cuts will be for the elderly.

In contrast, look at what happened in France in the past few 3
months. A new conservative government with a large parliamentary majority proposed what were very minor cuts in pensions and health care
provisions for public workers and very minor downsizings in some of
the state industries, such as railroads, to reduce France's budget deficit.
Those affected took to the streets, struck, snarled traffic and did everything they could to disrupt the French economy.

The public was deeply inconvenienced, but opinion polls showed 4
popular support for the protesters. The angry public employees were
not the political supporters of the parties in power, yet the pressures
they were able to generate became so intense that the government
eventually withdrew all of its proposed cutbacks.

A year or two earlier, the same thing happened at Air France, 5
when it proposed a downsizing plan very similar to those implemented
in America. The workers actively rebelled and the downsizing plan was
withdrawn.

Compare that with what happened when President Reagan fired 6
the air traffic controllers: Nothing.

Today, big, profitable companies that could easily pay employ- 7
ees their current wages and fringe benefits announce huge downsizings
(AT&T, with a 40,000-person reduction, being only the most recent).
What happens? Nothing.

The French exhibit social solidarity and fight back while Americans meekly accept their individual fates. 8

Reading about the successes of French workers, Americans comfort themselves with the idea that the French are being unreasonable and will eventually have to face the facts of global competition, technologies that no longer need unskilled workers and slow growth, and accept it as Americans have already. Even if that belief is true, every year that the demanded cutbacks can be delayed is one more year of good living for the French work force. Being the first to accept austerity is not smart unless it leads to something better later, and no one is promising Americans anything better. 9

The other American response is to point out that the United States has created a lot more jobs in the past quarter of a century than has Europe. That is certainly true, but countries with negative population growth like France do not have to create the almost 40 million new jobs that the United States has created. Official unemployment in Europe is almost double America's rate, but much of that difference is due to the way that Americans keep their unemployment numbers. Part-time workers who want full-time jobs (there are 4.5 million of them), for example, are counted as employed. 10

Unemployment benefits in much of Europe, certainly in France, are also higher than what one would earn in a minimum-wage job in the United States. As a result, France's unemployed enjoy a higher standard of living than many of those who got one of America's new jobs. A new job is a good thing only if it raises the worker's standard of living. 11

The bottom line is simple. If you are one of those American workers who has suffered from downsizing or reduced real wages, you clearly would be better off if you lived in France. 12

If one asks why the American and French reactions are so different, there is a simple answer. The two have very different beliefs about the roles played by the individual and the society in determining individual success or failure. Americans take individualism seriously. They are personally responsible for their own failures. They have no right to expect help from others. Anything given by others is an act of charity, not required, and ultimately demeaning to those who get it. 13

The French believe that much of the success or failure of life is caused by social organization. If something goes wrong in their lives, they are not necessarily to blame. Society hasn't done what it should have done—acted to create the condition and structures to improve their chances to succeed. Put bluntly, the French simply don't believe 14 in laissez faire. Economic conditions are not weather conditions that must be accepted. They are man-made and can be altered.

Because of American beliefs in individual responsibility to the exclusion of all else, America leads in rolling back the advances of the social welfare state even though social welfare is far less advanced in America than elsewhere. Since the Great Depression, Americans, like those in the rest of the wealthy industrial world, have come to expect that government should use educational programs to narrow earnings gaps and provide a social safety net for those the private economy does not want—the sick, the old, the unemployed. But under the proposals now being debated in Washington, all of that is to change. 15

America seems poised to go back to a 19th century variant of capitalism. Then, the English philosopher Herbert Spencer formulated a concept he called "survival of the fittest" capitalism (a phrase that Darwin eventually borrowed to use in his explanations of evolution). Spencer believed that it was the duty of the economically strong to drive the economically weak into extinction. That drive was in fact the secret of capitalism's strength. It eliminated the weak. 16

Spencer created the eugenics movement to stop the unfit from reproducing because he believed that this was simply the most humane way to do what the economy would do in a more brutal way if left to itself. In Spencer's view, all remedial social welfare measures simply prolonged and expanded human agony by increasing the population, who would eventually die of starvation. 17

The GOP's "contract with America" is very Spencerian in tone and offers a return to "survival of the fittest" capitalism. Many of its advocates are, of course, less honest than Spencer, denying that anyone will starve to death. In their view, no social safety net is necessary, because if the social welfare system is taken away, no one will fall off the economic trapeze. If individuals are forced to face the reality of starvation, everyone will knuckle down to work. Fear will make them work so hard, hold on so tight, that they won't fall off. 18

Spencer's views that individual defects lead to economic inadequacies that cannot be corrected by social actions are mirrored today in books such as "The Bell Curve," which suggests racial inferiority. They preach that those at the bottom of the economic system both deserve to be there and cannot be helped because of their personal inadequacies. 19

No one has ever tried survival-of-the-fittest capitalism for any extended period of time in the modern era. For social scientists, it will be an interesting experiment. For those being experimented upon, it will be painful. For those interested in social stability, the risks are high. 20

HOW THE MAIDS
FOUGHT BACK

Sara Mosle

■

"HOW THE MAIDS FOUGHT BACK" shows how individuals can work together through unions to improve working conditions and ensure a livable wage. Written by Sara Mosle for the New Yorker in 1996, this selection profiles the hotel employees union in Las Vegas.

"Organized labor," as Mosle points out, "has been in need of an image overhaul" for some time. Unions have existed in America since the 1790s, but they flourished in the later nineteenth- and early twentieth-centuries, only achieving power when laws were enacted that guarantee workers the right to organize and to use methods such as collective bargaining, boycotts, and strikes to resolve disputes with employers. As Mosle explains, employers are required by law to bargain with the union "in good faith." The National Labor Relations Board (N.L.R.B.) can sanction employers and union leaders for unfair labor practices; however, the power of unions depends not only on the law but also on popular support. In the previous essay, Lester Thurow reminds us that union support was at a low point in 1981, when there was no significant protest against President Reagan's decision to allow unionized air traffic controllers on strike to be fired. What do you think most Americans feel about unions today? Do you or does someone you know belong to a union? If you were an employee and felt you were being treated unfairly, how would you hope to resolve the problem?

Early on a Monday morning last fall, a thin white woman in her late fifties was bending over to dust the legs of a chair in a hotel room in Las Vegas. The thick pile of the room's blue carpet had been freshly vacuumed. The king-size bed was neatly made with a quilted blue comforter. The woman emptied the ashtray and wiped off the faux Queen Anne dresser.

There are ninety thousand hotel rooms in Las Vegas, and, on a typical eight-hour shift, a maid may clean as many as sixteen rooms. "You might go into a room and they done had a fight or sex, and it might take you hours," a former maid explained. "But you might go into a room and everything is nice and neat, and you can be in and out of there in fifteen minutes."

This particular room isn't actually in a Las Vegas hotel. It is on the second floor of a two-story federal housing project in west Las Vegas, a predominantly black part of town several miles from the Strip. The room, a replica of an old suite at the Flamingo Hilton, which donated the furnishings, is part of a small training school for hotel workers. Berenice Thomas, the housekeeping instructor, showed me around: "This is a real bathroom. We dirty it up. We put on hair and dirt—you know, lipstick, makeup, the real stuff. You can't teach people to clean in a clean room." The school is run by Culinary Workers Union Local 226, an affiliate of the Hotel Employees and Restaurant Employees International Union (HERE), which, in turn, is a member of the A.F.L.-C.I.O.

Maid's work in Las Vegas has become something of a high-tech industry, studied by teams of professionals, who have plotted, for instance, the most efficient routes through a room. "When I started as a maid," Thomas recalled, "I had a bucket with soap, and I had this big old brush, and I had to rub and scrub. Nowadays, they got everything so it's spray and wipe—they got the soap in the bottle and you spray it on and you wipe it and you rinse it off." The work is akin to that of an assembly-line worker's, and, as in many factories, it pays union scale.

Beyond the Strip and the strip houses, Las Vegas has a surprisingly stable middle-class community. To the union workers who live there, Las Vegas is not Lost Wages but the safe bet, the sure thing. Hattie Canty, who is sixty-two, worked for more than a dozen years as a union maid at the Maxim casino and hotel, just east of the Strip. She is now the president of Local 226. She hired Thomas to run the school's housekeeping program, which graduated more than four hundred maids last year. Over the last ten years, when organized labor has been suffering setbacks across the country, Canty's union, which represents hotel workers—cocktail waitresses, dishwashers, fry cooks, maids, and so forth—in nearly all of Las Vegas's major casino hotels, has more than doubled its membership. With nearly forty thousand members, it is the nation's fastest-growing local in the private sector. Although most of its members are women, Canty is the first woman to serve as a top officer. Previously, the union had been dominated by men from "the front of the house"—doormen, bellhops, and waiters, who held jobs involving more contact with tipping customers. As president, Canty has helped to bring new power and prominence to the women of "the back of the house."

Canty was "found" by a HERE organizer, Roxana Tynan, at the Maxim in 1989. Tynan, who is the daughter of the critic Kenneth Tynan, became interested in unions in the mid-eighties as an undergraduate at Yale, where she rallied student sympathy for a strike by the university's clerical workers. Their union, like Canty's, was affiliated with HERE, which provides support and services to its locals around the country. After Tynan graduated, HERE recruited her to be a union organizer and sent her to Las Vegas, where she worked for the next four years.

Organizers are barred from talking to workers on the job, except in the employees' dining room or break room; in non-union companies they have no right to be on the property at all. Consequently, Tynan had to find people who were already working in the hotels and were willing to support a union drive from within. "Organizing was the scariest job that I could have imagined," she recalls. "It's really awkward. You'll knock on the doors of total strangers. Then, at some point, most of the workers hate you, because you're asking them to do something that they really don't want to have to do"—that is, risk their jobs.

Technically, of course, all workers in the United States (with the exception of a few public employees) have the right to organize and bargain collectively with their employers, but, as a waitress in Las Vegas points out, "you say the word 'union' in a non-union place and you get fired. If you want to organize, you're really putting your neck on the line."

"In a way, as an organizer you're sent out to look for Christian saints," Tynan says. "And you find them, which is even more impressive—they're always out there." In her experience, she says, "women are always more willing to step forward in any kind of organizing, anytime, anywhere." She goes on, "Women are always braver, without question. I think it's partly because women have less of a problem with the notion of the collective good. They have fewer ego problems. Hattie was the lady that all the other housekeepers talked about. It was like, 'Go see Hattie.' As soon as I met her, I knew."

"I did maid's work for a long, long time," Canty said recently to a gathering of graduates of the union's training school. "It's a job that

I never will be ashamed of." Canty is an inspirational figure within the union, and her election to the presidency of her local reflects larger changes in labor nationally. Last August, Lane Kirkland, the president of the A.F.L.-C.I.O., gave up his office after sixteen years of what had come to be seen as increasingly moribund leadership. Two months later, delegates at the A.F.L.-C.I.O. convention in New York passed over Kirkland's handpicked successor and voted in John Sweeney, in the first openly contested election in the labor federation's history. Organized labor has been in need of an image overhaul. As one room-service worker in Las Vegas put it, "There's a social stigma about being in a union. Unions are viewed as lower class, and you have people all over the country who don't want to be in the lower-class club." In recent years, Las Vegas has been the site of mass demonstrations, reminiscent of the nineteen-thirties, in which thousands of workers, marching for higher pay, better health benefits, and improved working conditions, have flooded the streets, carrying picket signs and banners.

"I am blessed to live and work in Las Vegas," Hattie Canty told [11] me. She was born in rural Alabama, and moved with her family to California in 1956. They settled in Las Vegas in 1961, the year after official segregation was ended on the Strip. Hattie's husband supported the family by working in construction and, later, in trucking. Except for a yearlong stint as a maid at the Thunderbird, which has long since closed, Canty stayed at home, keeping house and taking care of the children—she eventually had ten of them. Then, in 1975, her husband discovered that he had lung cancer. "When he got sick," Canty recalls, "he knew he was going to die, and he'd say to me, 'I could die in peace if I knew you could take care of the family.' I would go and hide the mail. I didn't want him to see that we were two months behind on our bills." He died a few months later, at the age of fifty-four, just shy of their twentieth wedding anniversary, leaving Hattie with eight of their ten kids still at home, to support on her own.

At this point, Canty's story might have taken a predictable turn: [12] at best, a series of menial minimum-wage jobs that would have put her further in debt; at worst, dependence on welfare. But, living in Las Vegas, she was able to join the Culinary Workers Union and get a job earning a decent salary as a maid at the Maxim. (Today, a union maid earns nine dollars and twenty-five cents an hour, five dollars more than the minimum wage.) Over the next dozen years, Canty worked her way up to a better-paid position as an attendant in the hotel's uniform room—a job that her oldest daughter, Rhonda, now holds. In addition to her salary, Canty received health-care benefits and a pension that will enable her to retire a few years from now. "My house is paid for," Canty said. "I bought cars while I was a maid. I bought furniture, I bought the things I needed for my family while I was a maid. And the way I did it is through organized labor."

Labor got its foothold in Las Vegas with Al Bramlet, a flamboy- 13 ant union worker who arrived in Las Vegas in 1946 and made a deal with the Mafia. Bramlet promised to recruit workers to the remote desert town in return for union recognition and a few perks for himself. This arrangement lasted, essentially unchanged, until the mid-seventies. Howard Hughes pushed the Mafia out of town, and a few years later Bramlet turned up in the desert dead, stripped of his clothes and shot in the head and chest. (Despite the town's shady beginnings, the Culinary Union is now considered to be squeaky clean.) With Bramlet gone, the union's old leadership coasted, hardly aware of its own diminishing powers, until 1984, when union contracts with the hotels came up for renegotiation. When owners took a tough stance at the bargaining table, workers walked out. Heidi Hughes, an organizer in Las Vegas, explains, "Some cities haven't had a strike in forty years, but we've always had a history of fighting for the union in this town. We've had strikes all along." But, for the first time, a citywide strike didn't force the Strip to "go dark": management was able to keep the hotels open using scab labor. Although most owners settled after sixty-seven days, the strike lingered on at some places for more than a year, and the union lost six hotels. Glen Arnodo, a Las Vegas organizer, says, "Most workers assumed that it was the beginning of the end of the Culinary Union in Las Vegas."

Organizers expected management to try to bust the union once 14 and for all when contracts came up again in 1989, and they were right. The first showdown occurred at Binion's Horseshoe, a famous downtown gambling joint, run by Jack Binion, who refused to settle. In January of 1990, workers struck the casino. The strike dragged on for months, into the long, hot summer and through the fall. Arnodo recalls, "I think Binion thought that we'd eventually go away, but we never did go away." The picketers' persistence paid off. After nine and a half bitter months, Binion settled. The next battle was at the Frontier, one of the oldest casinos on the Strip.

The Frontier, which was remodelled in the late eighties, is now 15 a three-building complex with a fifteen-story mirrored-glass tower. It sits at an angle off the main drag, with a moatlike parking lot and one of the larger neon signs on the Strip. It is owned by Margaret Elardi and her two sons, Tom and John. They bought the place in 1988, just a few months before its Culinary Union contract expired. By law, the Elardis were required to bargain "in good faith" with the union to reach a new settlement, but after months of stalling the family hired Joel Keiler, a notorious union-busting lawyer. (Keiler, whom the National Labor Relations Board later suspended for a year from handling labor cases before it, no longer represents the Frontier.)

After a confrontation with the unions staged by Keiler, the Elardis 16 unilaterally declared an impasse and imposed their own work rules. Salaries for new employees were drastically reduced; workers were fired without cause; seniority rules were essentially abandoned. Women who had worked days suddenly found themselves on the graveyard shift. A forty-hour work week, on which paid vacations and holidays depended, was no longer guaranteed. The Elardis stopped deducting members' union dues from their paychecks, refused to contribute to the union's health-and-welfare fund, and, in July of 1991, suspended all contributions to the workers' pension plans. (The Elardis did not return calls requesting an interview.)

On the morning of September 21st, some five hundred and fifty 17 workers, members of the Culinary Union and three other unions, walked out. Four and a half years later, they are still on strike. During that time, not a single striker has crossed the picket line to go back inside, and, in a show of solidarity rarely seen in labor these days, Culinary Union members voted to double their dues to support the strike fund. Arnodo told me how workers' lives had changed over the course of the strike: "Ninety children have been born, seven people have died, many more have gotten married, and a few moved from town." Strikers have strategically set up "shacks," which look like newspaper kiosks, at points of heavy traffic on the hotel's periphery. They congregate at the shacks and pass out leaflets explaining the issues of the strike; a tape player blares voices of workers chanting inspirational slogans; and, at any given moment, a few workers walk between the stations, carrying their signs.

Geoconda Arguello-Kline, or Geo, as her friends call her, is one 18 of the picket captains at the Frontier. A forty-year-old former maid, who now works for the union, she is married and has three children. She has short black hair and dark skin. She was born in Nicaragua and moved to Miami in 1979. Her father had been a colonel in the Nicaraguan Army, and her family was fleeing the Sandinista revolution. In Nicaragua, Geo's family was upper middle class: "We had servants, people to take care of stuff." But in the United States, Geo told me, "we were suddenly a family who had nothing." She went on, "I could not get a good job. I worked under bad conditions—minimum wage, no health insurance—and I had no language skills for looking for better jobs. Twelve of us lived in an apartment with two rooms." Her brother moved to Las Vegas, and Geo followed: "I started working as a guest-room attendant"—or maid—"and I understood how here people were making more money, how they weren't scared to lose their jobs, how they had health care and health benefits. My daughter, she has health problems. She grows tumors in her body. If I was still living in Miami, I would have no money to take her to the doctor. Now it is completely different." Her father, the former colonel, holds a union job in town. "Not until the fight at this hotel did I understand that we were fighting for the whole community," Geo said. . . .

The ongoing strike at the Frontier in Las Vegas shows just how hard it is to sustain labor's gains, even in a strong union town. The solidarity of the strikers has done little to end the fight, even though the N.L.R.B. has repeatedly upheld the striking unions' charges: one judge, in finding the company's actions illegal, described the Frontier's efforts at bargaining as "surreal." Then, last September, the Ninth Circuit Court of Appeals overwhelmingly upheld the unions' position again. The court found the Elardis' appeal "frivolous," declared their imposition of new work rules and suspension of the pension plan illegal, and upheld dozens of charges of unfair labor practices. The Elardis were therefore obligated to make illegally dismissed workers "whole" by paying back wages and to restore unpaid contributions to the pension plan. The court also awarded the union double all costs and attorneys' fees incurred by the appeal. The Elardis will, in all probability, end up paying millions, but the cost to the strikers has been at least as high. For four and a half years, they've been without their regular jobs, and six months after the court handed down its verdict they are still walking the picket line.

"Women are the future of labor unions," Peggy Pierce, a food server at the Desert Inn in Las Vegas, told me. "I have no doubt that if the A.F.L.-C.I.O. concentrated its efforts on women, a new labor movement would happen." Pierce, who is forty-one, looks a little like the young Liza Minnelli. She has short black hair, fair skin, and enormous eyes. She works in room service, an area that women, by an unwritten rule, were once excluded from, because of the purported danger to them in delivering late-night snacks to guests' rooms. She said, "They think we might walk into a room and somebody might hand us a fifty-dollar tip, and, God knows, they wouldn't want that to happen! They're protecting us from higher wages." She added, "The only women in this country who are absolutely guaranteed to make the same amount of money as the men standing next to them doing the same work are women in unions. If you're not in a union and you're a woman and you work, you're getting screwed. That's seventy cents on the dollar and it's not coming out of union shops but out of the vast, non-union America."

The day I met Pierce, she had just been house-hunting. "Las 21 Vegas is the last place in America where a maid or a food server can afford a house on a forty-hour-week salary," she said. "The economics in Vegas *are* the union. We are the standard of living in this town. If I woke up tomorrow morning and the Culinary Union had disappeared, I would walk in to work and I'd be making the minimum wage and I would have no health insurance. There's not a casino owner on the Strip who doesn't grind his teeth when he has to write those checks for the pension plan and health-and-welfare. But they have to do it, because we *make* them."

When I asked women in Las Vegas . . . if they thought of them- 22 selves as feminists, none of them, except Peggy, said yes. Most of them seemed bewildered by the question. But when I changed the question slightly and asked them about activism more generally, they all saw the union as capable of transforming women's lives. One maid at the Desert Inn said, "You'll find women who were in bad situations, and they got involved in the union, and they left their bad situations, they got out of their bad situations."

One afternoon, I accompanied Hattie Canty to the Maxim. As she 23 stood outside the employees' entrance, she threw open her arms and said, "If I could, I'd just put my arms all around this hotel and give it a big hug and a kiss!" We were going to have lunch with Hattie's daughter Rhonda in the employees' dining room. As we walked toward the dining room, I noticed a woman wearing a button that read, "A woman's place is in the union." Canty mused, "You know, I think about this hotel a lot, and this is home. This is where I raised my family. In a sense, the Maxim was like a husband to me."

After lunch, Canty took me to the uniform room, in the hotel's 24 basement. It looked like a dry cleaner's. Long racks held rows of uniforms, organized by size and kind. Hattie showed me where she had worked. "This is the exact space. This is the same table that was in here, the same uniforms, just about everything that was here when I was here. A lot of my youth was spent here, and so my mark is here," she said. "It has not been a picnic for me, but I don't think I'd like to go on a picnic every day. I have enjoyed the struggle. I'm not the only Hattie. There's lots of Hatties out there."

WOMEN ON THE CORPORATE LADDER

Judith H. Dobrzynski

■

THIS ESSAY BY NEW YORK TIMES reporter Judith H. Dobrzynski shifts the focus from workers helping each other to employers helping their employees. She focuses specifically on policies designed to help women with families climb the corporate ladder — policies such as flexible work schedules, maternity and paternity leave, and access to child care. It may be too early to know how effective these policies will be, but Dobrzynski points out that women in companies with policies do not seem to be advancing any faster than women in companies that have done nothing to help.

Even though a July 1996 Foundation for Future Leadership study ("Gender Differences at Work: Are Men and Women Really That Different?" by Michael R. Perrault and Janet K. Irwin) shows that women do better than their male counterparts in twenty-eight of thirty-one categories evaluating management skills, women are still banging their heads against the so-called "glass ceiling." Dobrzynski refers to another study, by Catalyst research group, that shows how few women have risen to the highest echelon: Only 10 percent of the officers and 2 percent of the top-paid executives at Fortune 500 companies are women. These statistics reveal that women fare no better at the top of the ladder than they do at the bottom, where female blue-collar workers on the average earn only seventy-one cents for every dollar earned by a man in a comparable job.

Dobrzynski suggests that many of the corporate policies are not so much intended to help women advance as to move them into the highly controversial "Mommy track." What do you think should be done, if anything, to improve opportunities for women in the workplace?

I f only corporate America would make it easier for women to take care of their duties at home, they could at last compete on an equal footing with men in the workplace—and rise to the top.

That, at least, was the much heralded theory of the 1980s. A comparison of two recent reports suggests, however, that it is not working out that way in the 1990s.

One, a census of women at the top of corporate America, delivers the somber news that women hold just about 2 percent of the power positions no matter how they are defined—by title, by paycheck or by responsibility for the bottom line. Of the nation's 500 largest companies, only 61 can count a woman among their five top earners or can say that a quarter or more of their officers are women. Just 13 of the 61 can do both.

When a roster of those 61 companies is placed side-by-side with a list of companies that have won plaudits for their enlightened work-and-family policies, there is very little overlap: few companies that did well on the census conducted by Catalyst, a nonprofit women's research group, also shined on *Working Mother* magazine's list of the "100 Best Companies for Working Mothers," released in September. And vice versa.

Only a handful of companies—Avon Products; the Federal National Mortgage Association, or Fannie Mae, and Merck among them—proved to be exceptions, showing up on both lists.

"The lack of association" between the two lists, said Heidi Hartman, director of the Institute for Women's Policy Research in Washington, D.C., "suggests that this could be a problem."

Jean Lipman-Blumen, a professor at Claremont Graduate School in Claremont, Calif., and author of "Gender Roles and Power," also finds the contrast worrisome. "I think it means that the women who are making it are making it in the old-fashioned way, accepting the traditional organizational structure and culture," she said. "And it looks like the organizations that have made it easier for women to work in are substituting that for hard-nosed rewards at the top."

Right now, any conclusions about the significance of the two studies are pure conjecture because they are not comparable in approach, subject or measurement. Catalyst's census covered only companies on *Fortune* magazine's list of the 500 largest American corporations. *Working Mother* looked at a wider spectrum of companies—including some large law firms and advertising agencies, for example—when it rated pay rates, advancement opportunities, access to child care, flexibility in work schedules and other family-friendly benefits such as paid maternity and paternity leave.

Without research specifically studying the relationship between women's advancement and workplace policies, it is hard to say exactly what is happening in corporate America. But several experts said these two studies, while admittedly apples and oranges, did suggest a few hypotheses. 9

Women may simply be climbing the corporate ladder fastest in industries traditionally friendly to women, like cosmetics and retailing, and work-and-family policies may not be much of a factor at all in their advancement. On the other hand, Catalyst's list of companies where women are making good strides is diversified, ranging from Pitney Bowes to Corestates Financial Corporation. 10

It might be, instead, that some companies are putting one foot before the other. "These are different dimensions of women's advancement, and you need both," Ms. Hartman said. "The fact that some companies excel at one and not the other may mean they just got through one culture change first, that the Polaroids and the Xeroxes and the I.B.M.'s may have to develop family-friendly policies to get women up the pipeline, to keep them before they can promote them." If so, women may grow impatient, but they can have hope. 11

The divergence in lists might also spring from the difference between rhetoric and reality. "Some companies with a good reputation for policies on paper are not so good in practice," said Robin Ely, an associate professor at Columbia University who specializes in gender and race relations. "It can be perceived as a negative if you take advantage of these policies." At such companies, having family-friendly policies on the books would not matter one way or the other. 12

The most extreme theory is, in Ms. Hartman's words, the "paranoid" one. "It may mean what we always thought it meant," she said, "that family-friendly policies are a way to keep women in their place and not let them rise too far, that the policies that allow for advancement may also limit advancement." 13

Without further study, it is difficult to say which thesis is right. What is true at one company may not describe the situation at others. At any corporation, too, a combination of factors might be at work to allow or prevent women's advancement. 14

Nonetheless, many people familiar with corporate life lean toward the view that for women rising to the top remains incompatible with a 15 thriving family life. "To be successful in a lot of companies, a woman has to conform to the image of someone who doesn't have an outside life, who doesn't have a family, and who doesn't have any interests outside of work," Ms. Ely said. "We're not much better on this than we were a few years ago."

Men in high-powered jobs naturally point out that there are no special rules or policies allowing them to have better home lives; they accept that success in the corporate world is incompatible with attendance at every school play and soccer game. But women counter that expectations for them still differ considerably from those for men. "We don't ask men to distort their lives as much as we ask women to distort theirs," Ms. Lipman-Blumen said. "We expect men to have a traditional family, with the pictures on his desk, and that puts demands on women, too."

That is why, in the view of Dana Friedman, who co-founded the Families and Work Institute, a research group, "the Mommy track is alive and well."

The "Mommy track," of course, is the idea advanced in the late 1980s by the late Felice N. Schwartz, who founded Catalyst. She suggested that corporations defined a path in which women would take less demanding, lower-paying, more flexible jobs so they could also attend to children and family.

Although Ms. Schwartz said she had intended the Mommy track to be a voluntary and often temporary choice, critics protested the very idea. It was dangerous, they said, to say that women managers had to choose between career and family, while men could have both. Worse, critics complained, giving credence to a Mommy track would reinforce discrimination against women under a more sophisticated guise. Smart women were advised to ignore the Mommy track.

Companies apparently did not, however. Ms. Friedman, now a senior vice president at Corporate Family Solutions, a Nashville company that helps companies design work and family policies, said that today many companies were indeed equating the use of family-friendly policies, like flextime, with a move to the Mommy track.

Family-friendly companies may not, of course, have evil lurking in their hearts. "I don't know if the 'good' companies are doing it on purpose," Ms. Lipman-Blumen said. "I think they think they are doing great things for women. But that's the first step. They need to take the next."

"And," she added, "the other companies need to make life more livable for both men and women who want to get to the top."

But if the reasons are unclear, the lack of progress at the top is 23
not. "We're not better off than we were a few years ago," Ms. Ely said.
"It's not happening, except at the margins. Some big companies call me,
concerned about high turnover among women. They want me to come
and give a talk to senior managers. And then nothing happens."

The message to women is also transparent: "For most working 24
women, for those looking for a family life and to move up the corporate ladder," Ms. Friedman said, "this is not something the corporation
is going to make easy for you."

COLOR BLIND

Ellis Cose

■

IN THE PRECEDING ESSAY, JUDITH DOBRZYNSKI *looked at the effect of policies to help women climb the corporate ladder. Here, Ellis Cose examines corporate-sponsored affirmative action for African Americans. Cose has written many books including* The Rage of a Privileged Class *(1993),* A Man's World: How Real Is Male Privilege—and How High Is Its Price? *(1995), and* Color Blind *(1996), from which this selection was adapted for* Newsweek *magazine in November 1996.*

As you begin to read this essay, you will see that Cose mentions recent events involving three different corporations: Texaco, Denny's, and Shoney's. Cose explains a little about the last two, but he only refers to what he calls the "Texaco imbroglio." In a historic settlement to a race-discrimination lawsuit brought by 1,400 employees (and supported by a boycott led by the Rev. Jesse Jackson), Texaco agreed to invest $176 million in pay hikes and initiatives to hire, train, and promote African Americans, women, and other underrepresented minorities. In addition, Texaco plans to encourage diversity among its business partners by seeking contracts with minority- and women-owned businesses.

Cose's essay was published before the Texaco diversity plan was announced, but it might be interesting to speculate about his reaction, given what he says in this essay about other affirmative action plans. What are your reactions to the Texaco plan and to Cose's argument? What else do you know about the history and politics of affirmative action as it relates to work—for example, in regard to hiring or competition for government contracts?

In "The ethics of living Jim Crow," an autobiographical essay published in *Uncle Tom's Children* in 1940, Richard Wright told of his first job at an eyeglass lens-grinding company in Jackson, Mississippi. He landed the job, in part, because the boss was impressed with his education, and Wright was promised an opportunity to advance. "I had visions of working my way up. Even Negroes have those visions," wrote Wright. But even though he did his best to please, he discovered, over time, that nobody was teaching him a skill. His attempts to change that only provoked outrage. Finally, a co-worker shook his fist in Wright's face and advised him to stop making trouble: "This is a white man's world around here, and you better watch yourself."

Such sentiments obviously would not be openly voiced in most companies today. The civil rights revolution has seen to that. Still, it seems that every so often we get ugly reminders—of which the Texaco imbroglio is the latest—that Jim Crow's spirit is not yet dead. In 1994, Denny's restaurant chain agreed—in a settlement with the Justice Department—to put a civil rights monitor on its payroll and to cough up $45 million in damages, after a slew of complaints alleging discrimination against customers and employees. The previous year Shoney's, another restaurant chain, settled a suit for over $100 million that alleged, among other things, that managers were told to keep the number of black employees down in certain neighborhoods.

People of color with training and experience are "treated like s--t in too many places on the job," said assistant labor secretary Bernard Anderson, whose responsibilities include the Office of Federal Contract Compliance Programs. Even within the labor department, said Anderson, he had seen racial prejudice. When a black colleague, a Rhodes scholar, appointed two other blacks with impeccable credentials to positions, "the black lawyers were very empowered and encouraged by all of this," recalled Anderson, "but a number of the white lawyers . . . were just shaking in their boots." By and by, he said, a "poison pen memorandum" found its way around the department. The missive made insulting, scatological comments, questioned the credentials of the people who had been appointed, and declared that affirmative action had gone too far.

Resentment against minorities often surfaces in places where "diversity" or affirmative action programs are in place. And that resentment often breeds resistance that results not merely in nasty comments but in outright sabotage.

Some time ago, the black employees of a large, international corporation invited me to talk about a previous book, *The Rage of a Privileged Class*, at a corporate-wide event. In talking with my hosts, I quickly discovered that they were not merely interested in my insights. They wanted me to send a message to the management. They were frustrated because a corporate affirmative-action program, of which the management was extremely proud, was not doing them any good. Mid-level managers, it turned out, got diversity points for hiring or promoting minorities, but the corporation had defined minorities in such a way that everyone who was not a U.S.-born white man qualified. In other words, the managers got as much credit for transferring white men from Europe, Australia, and Canada as they did for promoting African Americans. And that is exactly what they were doing, according to the black employees, who wanted me to let the management know, in a nice and subtle way, that such behavior was unacceptable.

I'm not sure what message the management ended up extracting from my speech, but I am sure that the frustrations those black employees felt are widespread—and that the cause lies less in so-called diversity programs than in the widespread tendency to judge minority group members more by color than by ability.

Some two decades ago, I received a brutal lesson in how galling such attitudes can be. At the time, I was a young (maybe twenty-one or twenty-two years old) columnist-reporter for the *Chicago Sun-Times*. Though I had only been in the business a few years, I was acquiring something of a regional reputation. I hoped to break into magazine writing by garnering a few freelance assignments from *Esquire* magazine, so I had made an appointment with one of its editors.

The editor with whom I met was a pleasant and rather gracious man, but what he had to say was sobering. He wasn't sure, he confided, how many black readers *Esquire* had, but was reasonably certain the number was not high. Since I had not inquired about his readership, the statement took me a bit by surprise. I had been a longtime reader of *Esquire*, and it had never previously occurred to me that I was not supposed to be, that it was not me whom *Esquire* had in mind as an audience—never mind as a contributor. I don't know whether the editor bothered to read my clippings, but then, the clips were somehow superfluous; the very fact that I had written them made them so. All the editor saw was a young black guy, and since *Esquire* was not in need of a young black guy, they were not in need of me. I left that office in a state of controlled fury—not just because the editor had rejected me as a writer, but because he had been so busy focusing on my race that he was incapable of seeing *me* or my work.

A nominal commitment to diversity does not necessarily guarantee an appreciably better outcome, as I came to see several years ago when I was approached by a newspaper publisher who was in the process of putting together his management team. He was interested, he said, in hiring some minority senior managers, so I gave him some names of people who might be likely candidates. Over the next several months, I watched as he put his team in place—a team, as it turned out, that was totally white. Only after he had largely assembled that group did he begin serious talks with some of the nonwhites I had recommended. 9

I don't doubt the man's sincerity. He did want to hire some minority managers, and eventually did so. But what was clear to me was that to him, minority recruitment apparently meant the recruitment of people who couldn't be trusted with the organization's most important jobs. His first priority was hiring people who could do the work— meaning whites—and only after that task was complete would he concern himself with the window dressing of diversity. 10

Over the years, I have learned that affirmative action in theory and affirmative action in practice are two different things. In the real world it is much more than simply opening up an organization to people who traditionally have been excluded; it is attempting, usually through some contrived measures, to make organizations do what they don't do naturally—and it goes down about as easily as castor oil. Shortly after I announced my resignation as editor of the editorial pages of the New York *Daily News*, I took one of my white staff members out to lunch. He told me he had enjoyed working with me and was sorry to see me go. He had cringed when he heard that I was coming, he confided, for he had feared that I would be just another affirmative action executive, presumably incapable of doing the job competently. He admitted that he had been pleasantly surprised. 11

I was pleased but also saddened by his confession—pleased that he felt comfortable enough to tell me how he truly felt and saddened that the very fact that a person of color got a high-ranking job would lead him (as it had led so many before him) to question that person's credentials. Yet, having occasionally been the target of affirmative-action recruiters, I am fully aware that (whatever they may say in public) they don't always pay as much attention to credentials as to color. Therefore, I understand clearly why even the ostensible beneficiaries of such recruitment tactics may find affirmative action, as practiced by major corporations, distasteful and even offensive. A decade and a half ago, for instance, I received a call from an associate of an executive search firm who, after verbally tap dancing for several minutes, essen- 12 tially asked whether I wished to be considered for a job as a corporate director of equal opportunity. I was stunned, for the question made no sense. I was an expert neither on personnel nor on equal-employment law; I was, however, black, which seemed to be the most important qualification. I laughed and told him that I saw my career going in another direction. Still, I wondered just how serious the inquiry could be, since I seemed (to me, at least) so unsuited for the position. Since then, I have received other calls pushing jobs that have seemed every bit as outlandish.

At one point, a man called to discuss the presidency of a major 13 foundation. I confessed I didn't understand why he was calling me, and he assured me that the client was extremely interested in having me apply. The man's earnestness intrigued me enough that I sent him a resume. I never heard from him again, which confirmed, in my mind at any rate, that his interest was anything but genuine. I imagined him sitting in his office with a long list of minority candidates, from whom he would collect resumes and promptly bury them in a file, merely so that his clients would be able to say they had considered minorities. Indeed, when the foundation head was finally named (he was a white man with a long professional association with the foundation trustees), it was clear to me that the supposed search had been a sham. After one takes a few such calls, one realizes that the purpose is often defensibility ("Yes, we took a hard look at fifteen minority candidates, but none quite fit the bill") and that the supposed high-level position is merely bait to attract the interest of people who don't really have a shot—but in whom everyone must pretend they are interested because an affirmative-action program is in place.

It's logical to argue for the replacement of such shameful prac- 14 tices with something better—for some form of meritocracy. Yet affirmative-action critics who extol the virtues of a meritocracy generally ignore the reality of how a real-world so-called meritocracy works. If qualified, capable, and talented minorities and women exist, they say, corporations will reward them because they will recognize that it is within their economic interest to do so. That may well be true. But it is also true that effective executives are trained, not born. They come about because companies make an investment in them, in their so-called human capital, and nurture their careers along—and if corporations only see the potential in white men, those are the people in whom the investments are likely to be made.

John Kotter, a Harvard Business School professor and author of 15 *The General Managers*, discovered that effective executives generally benefited from what he called the "success syndrome." They were constantly provided with opportunities for growth: "They never stagnated for significant periods of time in jobs where there were few growth possibilities." The executives also, to be blunt about it, are often people of relatively modest intellectual endowment. They succeed largely because they are chosen for success.

A true meritocracy would do a much better job of evaluating and 16 choosing a broader variety of people. It would challenge the very way merit is generally imputed and, in giving people ample opportunity to develop and to prove themselves, it would create a truly level playing field.

Simply eliminating affirmative action would not bring such a true 17 meritocracy about. Indeed, a large part of the reason affirmative action is so appealing to so many people is that a meritocracy that fully embraces people of color seems out of reach; and affirmative action is at least one method to get people to accept the fact that talent comes in more than one color.

Yet, by its very nature, affirmative action is polarizing. Wouldn't 18 it be better, argue a growing number of Americans, to let it die in peace? A chorus of conservative critics even invoke the dream of Martin Luther King Jr. to make the case.

King would probably be more astonished than anyone to hear 19 that conservatives now claim him as one of their own, that they have embraced his dream of a color-blind world and invoke it as proof of the immorality and undesirability of gender and racial preferences. But even if he had a bit of trouble accepting his status as a general in the war against affirmative action, he would appreciate the joke. And he would realize that it is the fate of the dead to be reborn as angels to the living. King no doubt would be pleased to have new friends in his fight for justice, but he would approach them with caution. After sharing his disappointment over past alliances with people whose commitment to change did not match his own, King would address his new associates bluntly. "All right," he might say, "I understand why you oppose affirmative action. But tell me: What is *your* plan? What is *your* plan to cast the slums of our cities on the junk heaps of history? What is *your* program to transform the dark yesterdays of segregated education into the bright tomorrows of high-quality, integrated education? What is *your* strategy to smash separatism, to destroy discrimination, to make justice roll down like water and righteousness flow like a mighty stream from every city hall and statehouse in this great and blessed nation?" He might then pause for a reply, his countenance making it unmistakably clear that he would accept neither silence nor sweet nothings as an answer.

DEAD-END JOBS:
A WAY OUT

Katherine S. Newman

■

IN THIS PROPOSAL FROM The Brookings Review *(fall 1995), Columbia University anthropology professor Katherine S. Newman tries to convince corporate executives to help their own employees find better jobs in other firms. Her proposal comes out of a two-year comparative study of fast-food workers in Harlem and in Oakland, California. She determined that fast-food workers have great difficulty finding better jobs because they lack the "social networks" that would provide them with the kinds of information and referrals middle-class workers depend upon. Newman previously wrote a book on the problem of downward mobility in the middle-class titled* Falling from Grace *(1988).*

Mobility—downward or upward—is an important concept for thinking about work and career. It refers to the movement of an individual among job positions of varying quality. In "Dead-End Jobs," Newman focuses on the difficulty of moving from an entry-level, minimum-wage job to a position of greater responsibility and higher pay. Given what Ellis Cose in the preceding selection says about meritocracy ("effective executives are trained, not born") and what John Kotter says about the "success syndrome" (such executives "succeed largely because they are chosen for success" and constantly given opportunities for advancement), how do you think Cose would react to Newman's proposal? What do you think about it?

Millions of Americans work full-time, year-round in jobs that still leave them stranded in poverty. Though they pound the pave- 1 ment looking for better jobs, they consistently come up empty-handed. Many of these workers are in our nation's inner cities.

I know, because I have spent two years finding out what working 2 life is like for 200 employees—about half African-American, half Latino—at fast food restaurants in Harlem. Many work only part-time, though they would happily take longer hours if they could get them. Those who do work full-time earn about $8,840 (before taxes)—well below the poverty threshold for a family of four.

These fast food workers make persistent efforts to get better jobs, 3 particularly in retail and higher-paid service-sector occupations. They take civil service examinations and apply for jobs with the electric company or the phone company. Sometimes their efforts bear fruit. More often they don't.

A few workers make their way into the lower managerial ranks of 4 the fast food industry, where wages are marginally better. An even smaller number graduate into higher management, a path made possible by the internal promotion patterns long practiced by these firms. As in any industry, however, senior management opportunities are limited. Hence most workers, even those with track records as reliable employees, are locked inside a low-wage environment. Contrary to those who preach the benefits of work and persistence, the human capital these workers build up—experience in food production, inventory management, cash register operation, customer relations, minor machinery repair, and cleaning—does not pay off. These workers are often unable to move upward out of poverty. And their experience is not unusual. Hundreds of thousands of low-wage workers in American cities run into the same brick wall. Why? And what can we do about it?

STAGNATION IN THE INNER CITY

Harlem, like many inner-city communities, has lost the manu- 5 facturing job base that once sustained its neighborhoods. Service industries that cater to neighborhood consumers, coupled with now dwindling government jobs, largely make up the local economy. With official jobless rates hovering around 18 percent (14 people apply for every minimum-wage fast food job in Harlem), employers can select from the very top of the preference "queue." Once hired, even experienced workers have virtually nowhere to go.

One reason for their lack of mobility is that many employers in 6 the primary labor market outside Harlem consider "hamburger flipper" jobs worthless. At most, employers credit the fast food industry with training people to turn up for work on time and to fill out job applications. The real skills these workers have developed go unrecognized. However inaccurate the unflattering stereotypes, they help keep experienced workers from "graduating" out of low-wage work to more remunerative employment. . . .

As Harry Holzer, an economist at Michigan State University, has 7 shown, "central-city" employers insist on specific work experience, references, and particular kinds of formal training in addition to literacy and numeracy skills, even for jobs that do not require a college degree. Demands of this kind, more stringent in the big-city labor markets than in the surrounding suburbs, clearly limit the upward mobility of the working poor in urban areas. If the only kind of job available does not provide the "right" work experience or formal training, many better jobs will be foreclosed.

Racial stereotypes also weaken mobility prospects. Employers 8 view ghetto blacks, especially men, as a bad risk or a troublesome element in the workplace. They prefer immigrants or nonblack minorities, of which there are many in the Harlem labor force, who appear to them more deferential and willing to work harder for low wages. As Joleen Kirshenman and Kathryn Neckerman found in their study of Chicago workplaces, stereotypes abound among employers who have become wary of the "underclass." Primary employers exercise these preferences by discriminating against black applicants, particularly those who live in housing projects, on the grounds of perceived group characteristics. The "losers" are not given an opportunity to prove themselves. . . .

SOCIAL NETWORKS

Social networks are crucial in finding work. Friends and ac- 9 quaintances are far more useful sources of information than are want ads. The literature on the urban underclass suggests that inner-city neighborhoods are bereft of these critical links to the work world. My work, however, suggests a different picture: the working poor in Harlem have access to two types of occupational social networks, but neither provides upward mobility. The first is a homogeneous *lateral* network of age mates and acquaintances, employed and unemployed. It provides contacts that allow workers to move sideways in the labor market— from Kentucky Fried Chicken to Burger King or McDonald's—but not to move to jobs of higher quality. Lateral networks are useful, particularly for poor people who have to move frequently, for they help ensure a certain amount of portability in the low-wage labor market. But they do not lift workers out of poverty; they merely facilitate "churning" laterally in the low-wage world.

Young workers in Harlem also participate in more heterogeneous *vertical* networks with their older family members who long ago moved to suburban communities or better urban neighborhoods to become homeowners on the strength of jobs that were more widely available 20 and 30 years ago. Successful grandparents, great-aunts and uncles, and distant cousins, relatives now in their 50s and 60s, often have (or have retired from) jobs in the post office, the public sector, the transportation system, public utilities, the military, hospitals, and factories that pay union wages. But these industries are now shedding workers, not hiring them. As a result, older generations are typically unable to help job-hunting young relatives. 10

Although little is known about the social and business networks of minority business owners and managers in the inner city, it seems that Harlem's business community, particularly its small business sector, is also walled off from the wider economy of midtown. Fast food owners know the other people in their franchise system. They do business with banks and security firms inside the inner city. But they appear less likely to interact with firms outside the ghetto. 11

For that reason, a good recommendation from a McDonald's owner may represent a calling card that extends no farther than the general reputation of the firm and a prospective employer's perception—poor, as I have noted—of the skills that such work represents. It can move someone from an entry-level job in one restaurant to the same kind of job in another, but not into a good job elsewhere in the city. 12

Lacking personal or business-based ties that facilitate upward mobility, workers in Harlem's fast food market find themselves on the outside looking in when it comes to the world of "good jobs." They search diligently for them, they complete many job applications, but it is the rare individual who finds a job that pays a family wage. Those who do are either workers who have been selected for internal promotion or men and women who have had the luxury of devoting their earnings solely to improving their own educational or craft credentials. Since most low-wage service workers are under pressure to support their families or contribute to the support of their parents' households, this kind of human capital investment is often difficult. As a result, the best most can do is to churn from one low-wage job to another. 13

THE EMPLOYER CONSORTIUM

Some of the social ills that keep Harlem's fast food workers at the bottom of a short job ladder—a poor urban job base, increasing downward mobility, discrimination, structural problems in the inner-city business sector—are too complex to solve quickly enough to help most of the workers I've followed. But the problem of poor social networks may be amenable to solution if formal organizations linking primary and secondary labor market employers can be developed. An "employer consortium" could help to move hard-working inner-city employees into richer job markets by providing the job information and precious referrals that "come naturally" to middle-class Americans.

How would an employer consortium function? It would include both inner-city employers of the working poor and downtown businesses or nonprofit institutions with higher-paid employees. Employers in the inner city would periodically select employees they consider reliable, punctual, hard-working, and motivated. Workers who have successfully completed at least one year of work would be placed in a pool of workers eligible for hiring by a set of linked employers who have better jobs to offer. Entry-level employers would, in essence, put their own good name behind successful workers as they pass them on to their consortium partners in the primary sector.

Primary-sector employers, for their part, would agree to hire from the pool and meet periodically with their partners in the low-wage industries to review applications and follow up on the performance of those hired through the consortium. Employers "up the line" would provide training or educational opportunities to enhance the employee's skills. These training investments would make it more likely that hirees would continue to move up the new job ladders.

As they move up, the new hirees would clear the way for others to follow. First, their performance would reinforce the reputation of the employers who recommended them. Second, their achievements on the job might begin to lessen the stigma or fear their new employers may feel toward the inner-city workforce. On both counts, other consortium-based workers from the inner city would be more likely to get the same opportunities, following in a form of managed chain migration out of the inner-city labor market. Meanwhile, the attractiveness of fast food jobs, now no better reputed among inner-city residents than among the rest of society, would grow as they became, at least potentially, a gateway to something better.

14

15

16

17

ADVANTAGES FOR EMPLOYERS

Fast food employers in Harlem run businesses in highly compet-   18
itive markets. Constant pressure on prices and profit discourage them
from paying wages high enough to keep a steady workforce. In fact,
most such employers regard the jobs they fill as temporary placements:
they *expect* successful employees to leave. And despite the simple production processes used within the fast food industry to minimize the
damage of turnover, sudden departures of knowledgeable workers still
disrupt business and cause considerable frustration and exhaustion.

An employer consortium gives these employers—who *can't* raise   19
wages if they hope to stay in business—a way to compete for workers
who will stay with them longer than usual. In lieu of higher pay, employers can offer access to the consortium hiring pool and the prospect
of a more skilled and ultimately better-paying job upon graduation
from this real world "boot camp." The consortium could also provide
inner-city business owners with avenues of commerce and interaction
with firms and employers elsewhere in the city that might make possible new business ventures that prove valuable in their own right.

Consortiums would also appeal to the civic spirit of minority   20
business owners, who often choose to locate in places like Harlem
rather than in less risky neighborhoods because they want to provide
job opportunities for their own community. The big franchise operations mandate some attention to civic responsibility as well. Some fast
food firms have licensing requirements for franchisees that require
demonstrated community involvement.

At a time when much of the public is voicing opposition to heavy-   21
handed government efforts to prevent employment discrimination, employer consortiums have the advantage of encouraging minority hiring
based on private-sector relationships. Institutional employers in particular—for example, universities and hospitals, often among the larger
employers in East Coast cities—should find the consortiums especially
valuable. These employers typically retain a strong commitment to
workforce diversity but are often put off by the reputation of secondary-
sector workers as unskilled, unmotivated, and less worthy of consideration.

The practical advantages for primary-sector managers are clear.   22
Hirees have been vetted and tested. Skills have been assessed and cer-
tified in the most real world of settings. A valuable base of experience
and skills stands ready for further training and advancement. The con-

sortium assures that the employers making and receiving recommendations would come to know one another, thus reinforcing the value of recommendations—a cost-effective strategy for primary-sector managers who must make significant training investments in their workers.

MINIMAL GOVERNMENT INVOLVEMENT

Despite the evident advantages for both primary and secondary labor market employers, it may be necessary for governments to provide modest incentives to encourage wide participation. Secondary-sector business owners in the inner city, for example, might be deterred from participating by the prospect of losing some of their best employees at the end of a year. Guaranteeing these employers a lump sum or a tax break for every worker they promote into management internally or successfully place with a consortium participant could help break down such reluctance. 23

Primary-sector employers, who would have to provide support for training and possibly for schooling of their consortium employees, may also require some kind of tax break to subsidize their efforts at skill enhancement. Demonstration projects could experiment with various sorts of financial incentives for both sets of employers by providing grants to underwrite the costs of training new workers. 24

Local governments could also help publicize the efforts of participating employers. Most big-city mayors, for example, would be happy to shower credit on business people looking to boost the prospects of the deserving (read working) poor. 25

Government involvement, however, would be minimal. Employer consortiums could probably be assembled out of the existing economic development offices of U.S. cities, or with the help of the Chamber of Commerce and other local institutions that encourage private-sector activity. Industry- or sector-specific consortiums could probably be put together with the aid of local industry councils. 26

Moreover, some of the negative effects of prior experiments with wage subsidies for the "hard to employ"—efforts that foundered on the stigma assigned to these workers and the paperwork irritants to employers—would be reversed here. Consortium employees would be singled out for doing well, for being the cream of the crop. And the private-sector domination of employer consortiums would augur against extensive paperwork burdens. 27

BUILDING BRIDGES

The inner-city fast food workers that I have been following in 28
Harlem have proven themselves in difficult jobs. They have shown that
they are reliable, they clearly relish their economic independence, and
they are willing to work hard. Still, work offers them no escape from
poverty. Trapped in a minimum-wage job market, they lack bridges to
the kind of work that can enable them to support their families and
begin to move out of poverty. For reasons I have discussed, those
bridges have not evolved naturally in our inner cities. But where they
are lacking, they must be created and fostered. And we can begin with
employer consortiums, to the benefit of everyone, workers and employers alike.

A Proposal for a
WPA-Style
Jobs Program

William Julius Wilson

■

William Julius Wilson is a professor of social policy who has been study-ing the inner city for twenty-five years. Among the books he has written are The Truly Disadvantaged: The Inner City, the Underclass, and Pub-lic Policy *(1987) and* When Work Disappears: The World of the New Urban Poor *(1996), from which this selection is excerpted.*

Wilson argues in When Work Disappears *that being chronically un-employed deprives people of a routine that organizes their time, isolates them socially, contributes to their sense of inadequacy, and leads to despondency as well as anger. For these reasons, he believes that the government must step in where businesses and individuals have failed and create jobs that would enable the chronically unemployed to enter the job market for the first time or reen-ter it after a long hiatus.*

In "A Proposal for a WPA-Style Jobs Program," Wilson looks at three proposals offered by others and argues for the one that he thinks will work best. As you read, think about which proposal, if any, you prefer. Consider also the larger issue of whether the government has a legitimate role in helping solve problems such as chronic unemployment. As Wilson explains in this essay, the WPA was a large public works program begun in 1935 under President Franklin D. Roosevelt. Many people unemployed as a result of the Great De-pression were put to work building or improving roads, bridges, schools, li-braries, parks, and other public projects.

The central problem facing inner-city workers is not improv-ing the flow of information about the availability of jobs, or getting to where the jobs are, or becoming job-ready. The central problem is that the demand for labor has shifted away from low-skilled workers because of structural changes in the economy. . . .

Despite some claims that low-skilled workers fail to take advantage of labor-market opportunities (for example, Mead, 1992), available evidence strongly suggests not only that the jobs for such workers carry lower real wages and fewer benefits than did comparable jobs in the early 1970s, but that it is harder for certain low-skilled workers, especially low-skilled males who are not being absorbed into the expanding service sector . . . , to find employment today (Danziger and Gottschalk, 1995, Holzer, 1995, and Carlson and Theodore, 1995). As the economists Sheldon Danziger and Peter Gottschalk put it:

> In our view, the problem is not that more people have chosen not to work, but rather that demand by employers for less-skilled workers, even those who are willing to work at low wages, has declined. We find it paradoxical that so much attention has been focused on changing the labor-supply behavior of welfare recipients and so little has been given to changing the demand side of a labor market that has been increasingly unable to employ less-skilled and less-experienced workers. (1995, p. 156)

If firms in the private sector cannot use or refuse to hire low-skilled adults who are willing to take minimum-wage or subminimum-wage jobs, then the jobs problem for inner-city workers cannot be adequately addressed without considering a policy of public-sector employment of last resort. Indeed, until current changes in the labor market are reversed or until the skills of the next generation can be upgraded before it enters the labor market, many workers, especially those who are not in the official labor force, will not be able to find jobs unless the government becomes an employer of last resort. This argument applies especially to low-skilled inner-city black workers. It is bad enough that they face the problem of shifts in labor market demand shared by all low-skilled workers; it is even worse that they confront negative employer perceptions about their work-related skills and attitudes.

If jobs are plentiful even for less skilled workers during periods of economic expansion, then labor shortages reduce the likelihood that hiring decisions will be determined by subjective negative judgments concerning a group's job-related traits. Prior to the late 1970s, there was less need for the creation of public-sector jobs. Not only was economic growth fairly rapid during periods of expansion, but "the gains from growth were widely shared" (Danziger and Gottschalk, 1995,

p. 174). Before the late 1970s, public jobs of last resort were thought of in terms of "a counter-cyclical policy to be put in place during recessions and retired during recoveries. It is only since the late 1970s that the disadvantaged have been left behind during recoveries. The labor market changes . . . seem to have permanently reduced private sector demand for less-skilled workers."

Given the current need for public jobs to enhance the employ-   5
ment opportunities of low-skilled workers, what should be the nature of these jobs and how should they be implemented? Three thoughtful recent proposals for the creation of public jobs deserve serious consideration. One calls for the creation of public-sector infrastructure maintenance jobs, the second for public service jobs for less-skilled workers, and the third, which combines aspects of the first two, for WPA-style jobs of the kind created during the Franklin D. Roosevelt administration.

Edward V. Regan has advanced a proposal for a public-investment   6
infrastructure maintenance program. He points out that "infrastructure maintenance and upgrading can . . . benefit the economy by creating jobs, particularly for the relatively unskilled, and by raising productivity, thereby contributing to long-term economic growth" (1994, p. 43). According to one estimate, $1 billion spent on road maintenance will directly generate 25,000 jobs and indirectly put 15,000 people to work (Montgomery and Wyes, 1992). On the other hand, new construction creates fewer jobs at higher wages. Another study reports that new building projects or major construction employs 40 percent fewer workers than do maintenance projects (Wieman, 1993). Just as other low-skill jobs are made more attractive by programs of health care, child care, and earned income tax credits, so would low-skill jobs in infrastructure maintenance.

Aside from creating jobs, infrastructure maintenance could lead   7
to higher productivity. On this point, Regan states:

> Intuitively, fixing roads and bridges means less axle damage to trucks, fewer road mishaps and congestion, lowered costs of goods, and increased transportation productivity. Congested and deteriorated highways, broken water mains, inadequate sewage treatment, reduced transit services—all of these infrastructure deficiencies reduce productivity, drive up costs of goods and services, and inhibit people's access to employment. Any state or local government official who has tried to attract business facilities to a particular area and has watched business decision makers turn up their noses at cracked concrete and rusting bridges knows the practical meaning of those statements. (1994, p. 44)

Regan also points out that there are many other benefits stem- 8
ming from an improved infrastructure that are not accounted for in
standard economic measures, including shortened commuting times
and reduced traffic congestion. If well selected, public investment in infrastructure maintenance could contribute to economic growth. According to the Congressional Budget Office, the national real rate of
return for investments to maintain the current quality of the highway
system would be 30 to 40 percent, those involving selected expansion
in congested urban areas would be 10 to 20 percent (Regan, 1994).

Although the creation of infrastructure maintenance jobs will 9
provide some employment opportunities for low-skilled workers, the
condition of today's labor market makes it unlikely that many of these
jobs will actually go to high school dropouts or even to high school graduates with little or no work experience. To address this problem, the
economists Sheldon Danziger and Peter Gottschalk, in a recently published book, have advocated the creation of a labor-intensive, minimum-
wage public service jobs program of last resort for today's low-skilled
and jobless workers. They have in mind jobs such as day-care aides and
playground assistants who can supervise in school gyms and public
parks during after-school hours. These would be jobs for poor workers who cannot find a place in the private sector, jobs providing services
that the fiscally strapped cities can no longer afford to supply through
local resources.

Their plan for public service jobs differs in two important respects 10
from recent proposals aimed at increasing work requirements and work
incentives for recipients of welfare. First, their proposal is directed not
just at welfare recipients but at *all poor workers* adversely affected by current economic shifts, including those who have been ineligible for, or
who have chosen not to participate in, welfare. Only a small proportion of those whose labor-market prospects have diminished since the
early 1970s have been welfare recipients. Second, their proposal addresses changes in the demand side of the labor market by emphasiz-
ing work opportunities and earnings supplements rather than work requirements or incentives.

It is important to distinguish clearly the view of public service jobs 11
embodied in the proposal outlined in the Clinton administration's welfare reform plan that was pushed aside after the Republicans gained control of Congress in 1994. Under the Clinton proposal, welfare would
change from an entitlement to a transitional system through which
cash assistance would last only two years. For those welfare recipients
who reach the time limit but fail to find jobs in the private sector, tran-

sitional public-work slots would be made available. However, as Danziger and Gottschalk appropriately point out:

> A program offering jobs of last resort *only* to welfare recipients who exhaust two years of cash assistance would have the potential for perverse incentives and serious inequities. Families who either were not eligible for welfare or chose not to participate would not have access to these jobs. Even if the incentive to go on welfare in order to gain access to the [public service] jobs were small, offering jobs to welfare recipients but not to equally needy families who were trying to make it in the labor market could cause resentment. (1995, p. 173)

Danziger and Gottschalk recognize the fact that if programs provided "good" public-sector jobs, local officials would be tempted to fill them with displaced but experienced workers from manufacturing and other goods-producing industries. Therefore, workers with limited experience, skills, and training from high-jobless inner-city neighborhoods would very likely be passed over. Moreover, their proposal is designed to create public service jobs that produce goods and provide services that are not available in the private sector and would not displace private-sector workers.

Their proposal offers a subminimum-wage public service job to any applicant. They would set compensation at 10 to 15 percent below the minimum wage to encourage movement into private-sector jobs as they become available. Graduated job ladders would provide rewards to workers who succeed on the job, "but wages would always be lower than [that which] an equally successful worker would receive in the private sector" (Danziger and Gottschalk, 1995, p. 172). These wages would be supplemented with the expanded earned income tax credit and other wage supplements (including a federal child care subsidy in the form of a refundable income tax credit for the working poor and refundable state tax credits for the working poor).

The Danziger and Gottschalk proposal obviously would not provide a comfortable standard of living for the workers forced to take public service jobs. Such jobs are minimal and are "offered as a safety net to poor persons who want to work but are left out of the private labor market." However, they maintain that their proposal is an improvement over the current system, "which offers a minimum wage if you find a job, but leaves millions of poor persons searching for work and many others poor even though they have jobs" (1995, p. 173).

The final proposal under consideration here was advanced by the perceptive journalist Mickey Kaus of *The New Republic*. Kaus's proposal

183

is modeled on the Works Progress Administration (WPA), a large public works program announced in 1935 by Franklin D. Roosevelt in his State of the Union address. The public works jobs that Roosevelt had in mind included highway construction, slum clearance, housing construction, rural electrification, and so on. As Kaus points out:

> In its eight-year existence, according to official records, the WPA built or improved 651,000 miles of roads, 953 airports, 124,000 bridges and viaducts, 1,178,000 culverts, 8,000 parks, 18,000 playgrounds and athletic fields, and 2,000 swimming pools. It constructed 40,000 buildings (including 8,000 schools) and repaired 85,000 more. Much of New York City—including LaGuardia Airport, FDR Drive, plus hundreds of parks and libraries—was built by the WPA. . . . Lester Thurow has suggested that New York's infrastructure is now decaying because no WPA has existed to replace these public works in the half-century since. (p. 259)

Kaus advances what he calls a neo-WPA program of employ- 16 ment for every American citizen over 18 who wants it. The program would provide useful public jobs at wages slightly below the minimum wage. Kaus's proposed program would not only eliminate the need to provide public assistance or "workfare" for able-bodied workers but, unlike welfare, the WPA-style jobs would be

> available to everybody, men as well as women, single or married, mothers and fathers alike. No perverse "anti-family" incentives. It wouldn't even be necessary to limit the public jobs to the poor. If Donald Trump showed up, he could work too. But he wouldn't. Most Americans wouldn't. There'd be no need to "target" the program to the needy. The low wage itself would guarantee that those who took the jobs would be those who needed them, while preserving the incentive to look for better work in the private sector. (p. 125)

Kaus maintains that the work relief under his proposal, like the 17 work relief under Roosevelt's WPA, would not carry the stigma of a cash dole. People would be earning their money. Although some workers in the WPA-style jobs "could be promoted to higher-paying public service positions," most of them would advance occupationally by moving to the private sector. "If you have to work anyway," asks Kaus, "why do it for $4 an hour?"

Kaus's proposal would also place a time limit on welfare for able- 18 bodied recipients. After a certain date they would no longer be eligible for cash payments. However, unlike the welfare program proposed in 1995 by the Republican-controlled Congress, public jobs would be available to those who move off welfare. Kaus argues that to allow poor mothers to work, government-funded day care must be provided for their children if needed. But this service has to be integrated into the larger system of child care for other families in the United States to avoid creating a "day-care ghetto" for low-income children.

In Kaus's proposal the WPA-style jobs would be supplemented   19
with the earned income tax credit, which could be expanded at reasonable cost to lift all poor working families who work full-time throughout the year out of poverty. Because this subsidy would augment the income of all low-wage workers, those in low-level private-sector jobs would not be treated unfairly and their wages on average would be slightly higher than those in the guaranteed subminimum-wage public jobs.

Kaus maintains that there will be enough worthwhile WPA-style   20
jobs for anyone who wants one. The crumbling infrastructure in American cities has to be repaired. Services cut back by the government for financial reasons, such as picking up trash two times a week and opening libraries every evening and on Saturdays, could be reinstated. Jobs for men and women could range from filling potholes and painting bridges to serving as nurse's aides, clerks, and cooks. "With a neo-WPA maintaining highways, schools, playgrounds, and subways, with libraries open every evening and city streets cleaned twice a day, we would have a common life more people would find worth reclaiming" (p. 137).

In reviewing these three proposals, the Kaus neo-WPA jobs plan   21
is the most comprehensive because it would include not only the kind of infrastructure maintenance advocated by Regan but also the labor-intensive public service jobs proposed by Danziger and Gottschalk. And unlike the program proposed by Danziger and Gottschalk, neither Kaus's WPA-style jobs program nor Regan's infrastructure maintenance program would be targeted to poor workers. Whereas Kaus explicitly states that the pay scale for the neo-WPA jobs would be set below the minimum wage, Regan does not address the question of pay scale for his infrastructure maintenance jobs. It is reasonable to assume, however, that the pay scale for the infrastructure maintenance jobs would be lower than that for comparable levels of employment in the private sector. Nonetheless, both of these programs would very likely attract a substantial number of displaced experienced workers willing to take lower-paying public-sector jobs until they find higher-paying work in the private sector.

Given the broader scope of Kaus's neo-WPA jobs program, a   22

higher proportion of workers with few skills and little or no work experience would be employed than would be possible under the Regan
program of infrastructure maintenance. Accordingly, Kaus's program
would provide many more job opportunities for workers in high-jobless
inner-city ghetto neighborhoods.

The labor-intensive public service jobs program advanced by   23
Danziger and Gottschalk is designed to generate immediate employment opportunities for workers with low skills and little or no work experience. However, since it is explicitly aimed at poor workers, it runs
the risk of carrying a stigma. The WPA-style jobs advocated by Kaus
avoid this problem. The program would be presented as offering jobs
to any American who wants a job. Given the subminimum-wage scale,
it is likely to attract only a handful of workers who could readily find
higher-paying jobs in the private sector. And even if local authorities
succumbed to the temptation to fill the "good" WPA jobs with displaced
experienced workers, there would still be a sufficient number of labor-
intensive jobs requiring little skill, training, or experience. Moreover,
the experienced and higher-paid workers who accept WPA-style jobs
because of layoffs in the private sector would be likely to remain in the
program for only a short period of time.

Furthermore, the Kaus program of WPA-style jobs would lend   24
itself to the kind of progressive public rhetoric . . . that focuses on
problems afflicting not only the poor but the working and middle
classes as well. Thus, the program would promote social and economic
improvements benefiting all groups in society, not just the truly disadvantaged segments of the population. This is consistent with my argument that the joblessness of the poor, including the inner-city poor,
represents the more extreme form of economic marginality experienced by large segments of the population and stems in large measure
from changes in the organization of the economy, including the global
economy.

Because it is comprehensive, less likely to carry a stigma, and   25
lends itself to a progressive public rhetoric of social reform, I include
the Kaus neo-WPA jobs plan in my package of proposed immediate solutions to the jobs problem. However, there is the problem of admin-
istering a neo-WPA program, which is not discussed by Kaus. This program must be administered by the federal government (as was the
earlier WPA program under the Roosevelt administration) in order to
avoid the problem of "fiscal substitution"—that is, the shifting of
spending on public employment projects from the local or state level
to the federal government. This problem accompanied the implemen-

tation of the Comprehensive Employment and Training Act (CETA). The creation of public service employment through CETA in the 1970s did very little to increase the *aggregate* number of jobs in the economy because states and localities over time used the program to substitute subsidized positions for previously nonsubsidized public service jobs (Danziger and Gottschalk, 1995). This had the effect of shifting jobs from one funding source to another. Our goal here is to increase the number of jobs, and thus broad federal oversight is required.

As another way to avoid the problem of worker displacement, I would also recommend that the workers in the federal WPA-style program only produce goods and services that are not being produced in the private sector and are not presently provided by regular public-sector workers (Danziger and Gottschalk, 1995). If this problem is not addressed, considerable opposition to such a program could arise from both private- and public-sector unions and from businesses in the private sector. Accordingly, following Kaus, I have in mind useful public work that is currently not being done for financial reasons. This would include regular infrastructure maintenance; the cleaning of streets twice, not once, a day; the collection of trash twice a week instead of once a week; the opening of libraries on Saturday and in the evenings; the cleaning of municipal parks, playgrounds, and other public facilities at a level and with a frequency that would ensure their attractiveness and invite use; and the supervision of public playgrounds that would maximize safer, adult-sponsored recreation for all neighborhood children.

It is reasonable to anticipate that as WPA-style workers are used to replenish or revitalize public service staffs, certain states and localities might be tempted to scale back their regular workforce during periods of severe fiscal constraints and rely more on subsidized public service workers. To discourage this type of displacement of regular government workers, I would recommend that one WPA worker be removed for every regular worker's slot that is eliminated or not filled within a certain time period.

A WPA-style jobs program will not be cheap (see Danziger and Gottschalk, 1995 and Kaus, 1992). In the short run, it is less expensive to give people cash welfare than it is to create public jobs. Including the costs of supervisors and materials, it is estimated that each subminimum-wage WPA-style job would cost at least $12,000. That would represent $12 billion for every 1 million jobs created. This figure does not include additional funds to augment the subminimum wage from the earned income tax credit, nor does it reflect any long-run national real rate of re-

26

27

28

turn for public investment in infrastructure maintenance that would contribute to economic growth. . . .

[These] specific recommendations for immediate action would address the employment problems of many low-skilled workers, including those from the inner city. They would confront the current and serious problem of the disappearance of work in the inner-city ghetto. The jobs created would not be high-wage jobs but, with universal health insurance, a child care program, and earned income tax credits attached, they would enable workers and their families to live at least decently and avoid joblessness and the problems associated with it.

29

References

Carlson, Virginia L., and Nikolas C. Theodore. 1995. *Are There Enough Jobs? Welfare Reform and Labor Market Reality.* Illinois Job Gap Project, Center for Urban Economic Development, University of Illinois, Chicago.

Danziger, Sheldon H., and Peter Gottschalk. 1995. *America Unequal.* Cambridge: Harvard University Press.

Holzer, Harry. 1995. *What Employers Want: Job Prospects for Less-Educated Workers.* New York: Russell Sage.

Kaus, Mickey. 1992. *The End of Equality.* New York: Basic Books.

Mead, Lawrence. 1992. *The New Politics of Poverty: The Working Poor in America.* New York: Basic Books.

Montgomery, Michael, and David Wyes. 1992. "The Impact of Infrastructure." *DRI/McGraw-Hill U.S. Review,* October.

Regan, Edward V. 1994. *Infrastructure Investment for Tomorrow.* Public Policy Brief, no. 141, Jerome Levy Economics Institute, Bard College.

Wieman, Clark. 1993. "Road Work Ahead." *Technology Review* 96 (January): 42–48.

LET AMERICA
BE AMERICA AGAIN

Langston Hughes

■

We conclude with another poem by Langston Hughes (his "Theme for English B" opened Part I). "Let America Be America Again," which was first published in 1938 during the Great Depression, leads us to reflect on the American dream and its promise. This is a song of praise, an anthem to the hope that America symbolizes. But it also reproves us for allowing the dream to slip away from so many Americans while encouraging us to rededicate ourselves to making the dream a reality for all Americans.

As you think about the poem, turn your eyes to the future and contemplate what you want America to become in the twenty-first century. What opportunities for work and career do you foresee in the coming years? How will the future make it possible for us to fulfill ourselves as individuals? How can we use our diversity to strengthen our community?

Let America be America again.
Let it be the dream it used to be.
Let it be the pioneer on the plain
Seeking a home where he himself is free.

(America never was America to me.)   5

Let America be the dream the dreamers dreamed—
Let it be that great strong land of love
Where never kings connive nor tyrants scheme
That any man be crushed by one above.

(It never was America to me.)   10

O, let my land be a land where Liberty
Is crowned with no false patriotic wreath,
But opportunity is real, and life is free,
Equality is in the air we breathe.

(There's never been equality for me,   15
Nor freedom in this "homeland of the free.")

Say who are you that mumbles in the dark?
And who are you that draws your veil across the stars?

I am the poor white, fooled and pushed apart,
I am the red man driven from the land.   20

I am the refugee clutching the hope I seek—
But finding only the same old stupid plan
Of dog eat dog, of mighty crush the weak.
I am the Negro, "problem" to you all.
I am the people, humble, hungry, mean—   25
Hungry yet today despite the dream.
Beaten yet today—O, Pioneers!
I am the man who never got ahead.
The poorest worker bartered through the years.
Yet I'm the one who dreamt our basic dream   30
In that Old World while still a serf of kings,
Who dreamt a dream so strong, so brave, so true,
That even yet its mighty daring sings
In every brick and stone, in every furrow turned
That's made America the land it has become.   35
O, I'm the man who sailed those early seas
In search of what I meant to be my home—
For I'm the one who left dark Ireland's shore,
And Poland's plain, and England's grassy lea,
And torn from Black Africa's strand I came   40
To build a "homeland of the free."

The free?
Who said the free? Not me?
Surely not me? The millions on relief today?
The millions who have nothing for our pay   45
For all the dreams we've dreamed
And all the songs we sung

And all the hopes we've held
And all the flags we've hung,
The millions who have nothing for our pay —   50
Except the dream we keep alive today.

O, let America be America again —
The land that never has been yet —
And yet must be — the land where *every* man is free.
The land that's mine — the poor man's, Indian's, Negro's, ME —   55
Who made America,
Whose sweat and blood, whose faith and pain,
Whose hand at the foundry, whose plow in the rain,
Must bring back our mighty dream again.

    O, yes,   60
    I say it plain,
    America never was America to me,
    And yet I swear this oath —
    America will be!

Acknowledgments

Jenny Lyn Bader. "Larger Than Life" by Jenny Lyn Bader. Copyright © 1994 by Jenny Lyn Bader. From *Next: Young American Writers on the New Generation* by Eric Liu. Reprinted by permission of the author and W. W. Norton & Company.

Robert N. Bellah, Richard Madsen, William M. Sullivan, Ann Swidler, and Steven M. Tipton. "Finding Oneself through Work" from *Habits of the Heart.* Originally titled "Work" from chapter called "Finding Yourself." Copyright © 1985 by Robert N. Bellah, Richard Madsen, William M. Sullivan, Ann Swidler, and Steven M. Tipton. Reprinted by permission of University of California Press.

Nell Bernstein. "Goin' Gangsta, Choosin' Cholita: Claiming Identity." Originally titled: "Goin' Gangsta, Choosin' Cholita." Copyright © 1994 by Nell Bernstein. Reprinted by permission of the author, editor of *YO!* (Youth Outlook), a youth newspaper produced by Pacific News Service.

H. G. Bissinger. "Dreaming of Heroes," pages 73–79 from *Friday Night Lights* by H. G. Bissinger. Copyright © 1990 by H. G. Bissinger. Reprinted by permission of Addison-Wesley Publishing.

Dorothy Chin. "The Internet Encourages Isolation." Copyright © 1996 by Dorothy Chin. Originally titled "The Internet Can Only Encourage Further Isolation." This essay first appeared in the *Los Angeles Times*, May 25, 1996. Reprinted by permission of the author.

J. California Cooper. "How, Why to Get Rich," from *The Matter of Life* by J. California Cooper. Copyright © 1991 by J. California Cooper. Used by permission of Doubleday, a division of Bantam Doubleday Dell Publishing Group, Inc.

Ellis Cose. "Color Blind." Excerpt adapted from *Color Blind* by Ellis Cose. This excerpt appeared in *Newsweek*, November 11, 1996. Copyright © 1996 by Ellis Cose. Reprinted by permission of HarperCollins Publishers, Inc.

Judith H. Dobrzynski. "Women on the Corporate Ladder." The *New York Times*, November 6, 1996. Copyright © 1996 by The New York Times Co. Reprinted by permission.

Amitai Etzioni. "The New Community," pages 116–22 from *The Spirit of Community* by Amitai Etzioni. Copyright © 1992 by Amitai Etzioni. Reprinted by permission of Crown Publishers, Inc.

Barbara Garson. "McDonald's—We Do It All for You" from chapter 1 of *The Electronic Sweatshop* by Barbara Garson. Copyright © 1989 by Barbara Garson. Reprinted with the permission of Simon & Schuster.

Neil Howe and Bill Strauss. "Chutes and *(No)* Ladders" excerpt from chapter 14 of *13th Gen: Abort, Retry, Ignore, Fail?* Copyright © 1992 by Neil Howe and Bill Strauss. Reprinted by permission of Vintage, a division of Random House, Inc.

Langston Hughes. "Theme from English B" from *Collected Poems* by Langston Hughes. Copyright © 1994 by The Estate of Langston Hughes. Reprinted by permission of Alfred A. Knopf, Inc. "Let America Be America Again" from *Collected Poems* by Langston Hughes. Copyright © 1994 by the estate of Langston Hughes. Reprinted by permission of Alfred A. Knopf, Inc.

Shirley Jackson. "The Lottery" from *The Lottery.* Copyright © 1949 by Shirley Jackson. Copyright renewed © 1977 by Laurence Hyman, Barry Hyman, Mrs. Sarah Webster and Mrs. Joanne Schnurer. Reprinted by permission of Farrar, Straus & Giroux, Inc.

Acknowledgments

Submitting Papers for Publication

To Students and Instructors

We hope that we'll be able to include essays from more colleges and universities in the next edition of the *St. Martin's Guide to Writing* and our accompanying anthology, *Sticks and Stones and other student essays.* Please let us see essays written using *The St. Martin's Guide* you'd like us to consider. Send them with this Agreement Form to *The Guide*, Bedford/St. Martin's, 33 Irving Place, New York, NY 10003.

Instructor's Name _____

School _____

Address _____

Department _____

Student's Name _____

Course _____

Writing activity the paper represents _____

This writing activity appears in chapter(s) _____
of *The St. Martin's Guide to Writing*

Agreement Form

I hereby transfer to Bedford/St. Martin's all rights to my essay,

(tentative title), subject to final editing by the publisher. These rights include copyright and all other rights of publication and reproduction. I guarantee that this essay is wholly my original work, and that I have not granted rights to it to anyone else.

Student's signature: _____

Please type

Name: _____

Address: _____

_____

Phone: _____ E-mail: _____